AF326718

A MOTHER'S PRAYER

Steve Rand

Burlington, Vermont

Cover and layout design by Riley Earle

Onion River Press
89 Church Street
Burlington, VT 05401
info@onionriverpress.com
www.onionriverpress.com

Hardcover ISBN: 978-1-966607-39-7
Library of Congress Control Number: 2026903203

This book is dedicated to my brother, sister, and our children. May our mother and your grandmother no longer be just a ghost in the corner of our minds.

We must discover the extraordinary in ordinary people.

Greg Sharrow
a dear friend and mentor

Ann Rand
1944–1984

PREFACE

Bruises   Scars   Tumors
riddle us all

take a breath for hesitation
mold an image with a word

speak to this pain
this spoiled body

make no demands
only engender memories

those sojourns to the center
of your life

Keepsakes   Gifts   Peace
heal us all

unbury your first memory of grace
something as holy as you

touch the edges of time
and call out

call out for the mercy of all
unpleasantries

caught in your net of time
like creatures

Stories   Songs   Prayers
unburden us all

"Why are we going to church?"

It was a midweek morning during summer vacation, and I was missing a kickball game—free and fun recreation for all of us kids in our neighborhood.

"I need to confess my sins, and you, do too, Steve," my mother said, taking her eyes off the road to smile at me momentarily. Her dimples curled. Her ivory teeth glistened.

"Confess? Why?"

"Because I want to go to Heaven, and you should too," my mother answered quickly, glancing at me with another broad and winsome smile.

"How do you know Heaven exists?" At eleven years old, I knew only of Heaven as a place where dreams might, if I remained free of sin, come true. But on this morning, that place, where wonderful things most certainly occurred absent of sin, was my elementary school gym, a place where my friends were running around, kicking and dodging and throwing a rubber red ball furiously. I was skeptical about dreams materializing in an empty, musty church, where the oppressive smell of frankincense and myrrh would certainly cling to my clothes for the rest of the day, reminding me that play and church differed greatly.

"I don't know if Heaven exists," my mother said. She did not smile this time. She was fixated on the road ahead, surrounded by sluggish cars scorched by a sweltering sun.

We were in a 1977 Ford LTD, a behemoth mound of brown-coated metal barely controlled by my mother, who rarely drove while she was married to my father, making her experience of driving a car with power steering profoundly limited. She liked to grip the steering wheel at the eleven and one o'clock positions instead of the preferred ten and two o'clock. This made her knuckles look like teeth biting into the sun-baked dash. With her body only inches from the steering wheel, wearing bug-eyed sunglasses of the '70s, which she loved and would not be seen in public without, my mother looked like a praying mantis piloting a battleship. When she drove, the car swayed to and fro, drifting across the median, buoyed by some mysterious force. I did not have the heart to tell her that I felt far safer when my older sister, Chris, who had just received her learner's permit, drove the battleship. Such a proclamation would have caused more injury to an already broken heart. Plus, I often thought the mysterious force that kept the car from careening off the road while my mother drove had something to do with her indefatigable belief in a higher power and her longing to be free of sin.

Dutiful. That was my mother, Anne Rose Morrell Rand, a devout Catholic, who believed entrance into such a precious kingdom—a wondrous paradise in her mind—must be earned with conviction. So she prayed ceaselessly: in the morning before her low-wage work as a secretary for the local community college; in the car while delivering her three exuberant children to sporting events; during dinner after preparing a meal that drained the last of her day's vitality. Just before bed, when it was quiet and dark, she prayed steadfastly, prayed unshakably, prayed passionately. She liked to kneel, with her arms worn like frayed ropes, tethering her body to a neatly arranged bed about to absorb the last of her sweat, and incant *Hail Marys*. Her forehead resting against her thumbs. Her hands clasping a rosary dangling like a lure. Her prayers were in her eyes, in her gait, and in her dreams of an everlasting life.

"Why go to church if Heaven does not exist?" I was flummoxed, twisting a Rubik's Cube in the front seat of the brown battleship next to my mother, my towhead barely above the dashboard, glancing from the cube of colors to a bright, summer-day sun, wondering if Heaven had night and day or if I would ever see an angel fall from the sky. I imagined angels often, mostly at night, after praying, and just before sleep. They played on the walls—shadowy wisps encircling my younger brother and me—dancing in the moonlight like marionettes on strings, prancing and jigging to the whims I conjured.

"I go to church to remind myself that I do not need to know for sure that Heaven exists. I just need to have faith that it does." My mother turned into the parking lot of Immaculate Heart of Mary, a small Roman Catholic church made of red bricks near our house in Corning, New York. The car lacked grace as it bounced into an empty space. My mother parked near the entrance and stashed her sunglasses in her purse. Then she looked at me. "Let's go to confession, then meet with Father Rogers about you becoming an altar boy."

~

My mother went to confession many times in the months following my father's departure. Before he left, he really did not have much to say. But my mother did. She was in a state of shock after he told her that he was leaving, fleeing to California with his secretary. She called my father names I had never heard before.

"How could you do this? How could you leave us?" Mom's voice was convulsive and gravelly.

My father did not answer her questions. He moved toward Mom as if to hug her, as if his entire body were a peace offering.

My parents were in the kitchen, near a spotless sink. Dark, faux-wood cabinetry and a white laminated countertop separated them from my sister, brother, and me. We were sitting at an oblong kitchen table, inhaling all the anguish of a father's flight. My father's arms and my mother's back were all I could see. The cabinets obscured my view of his slender nose that held his wire-rimmed glasses and her brown-haired head with a few strings of gray. She moved slightly to her right, avoiding my father's embrace.

"No. No. No," Mom cried.

Then I heard a dull thump, and my mother fell listlessly to the floor.

My sister, brother, and I vaulted quickly out of our chairs and sprinted to her. She was sprawled on the pale linoleum floor, unconscious; her head tilted, her breathing shallow. My father stood above the four of us. His left hand rested on the counter next to a large glass casserole dish. We shook our mother vigorously, pushing and prodding her body.

"Wake up! Wake up!"

My father stood stock-still with stunned eyes and his mouth agape. Then my fifteen-year-old sister rose from my mother's side and started striking our father wildly with her arms and fists. She kept slamming our father's chest and screaming incoherently into his face. Her rage could not move him. Her tears could not move him. He stood motionless with dispassionate eyes as Chris pushed and shook and struck his shoulders. He remained undisturbed as if he were stuck in quicksand, accepting his fate, allowing the earth under his feet to slowly swallow him whole.

"Leave! Go! Leave us!" Chris demanded as her enormous sobs swelled in her cheeks.

My father moved away from his daughter, from his wife and two sons, dragging his body to the kitchen table, where he sat and began sobbing uncontrollably with his face buried in the palms of his hands, obscuring his shame. His shoulders slouched. He began to cough and choke as his pain and his brutishness spilled onto his own hands. He wept and he wept and he wept only a few feet away from his children, from his suffering wife, who began to stir slowly and regain consciousness.

We sat Mom up and leaned her back against the kitchen cabinets. Her head wobbled, so my brother and I each held a shoulder, pinning our mother against the cabinets while my sister gathered ice, wrapped the cubes in a dishtowel, and placed it on top of our mother's head. Her long, brown lashes fluttered as her deep blue eyes searched our faces for revelations. Her usually rosy cheeks were ashen.

"What happened?"

We did not say anything.

"My head hurts." My mother closed her eyes and grimaced. "Where is your father?"

My father suddenly came around the corner, stood at the edge of the kitchen counter, and looked down at the four of us. His eyes were red and swollen and vacant.

"What happened?" my mother asked again.

My father remained silent, immobile, his arms drooping below his waist.

My mother forced herself onto her feet as one hand held the towel with ice and the other hand purchased the edge of the counter. She noticed the open cabinet and the glass casserole dish.

"Did you hit me?" She turned to face my father. "Were you trying to kill me?"

My father again said nothing. He only sniveled and blinked.

The silence lasted beyond the pained expression on Mom's face, where veins quivered under azure eyes. She dropped the towel and ice to the floor then charged at my father.

"You tried to kill me!" She pushed and prodded and thump-ed his chest relentlessly. My father stumbled and shuffled and blindly grabbed at the front door behind him.

"Get out! Get out! And don't come back!"

My mother drove him out of the house. My father did not resist. He did not say goodbye. He looked bewildered. Then the door closed. My mother turned, put her back against the front door of the two-story, gray ranch house that she had furnished with her husband's money, and collapsed to the floor, wailing, praying, grieving. We huddled around her and wailed and prayed.

Bits of daylight leaked into the hallway, and I began to imagine pallid, somber angels forming from particles of dust gathering above our heads while we wept, consoling each other without words. My mother rose and pulled us to our feet. Large teardrops hung from her long lashes. She hugged us tightly, and we buried our heads into her battered body. There was only haziness as I pressed my face into her shoulder. I felt her tears on my scalp, gentle kisses on my warm, fleshy cheeks. Then she let go, and I watched her walk into the kitchen. She effortlessly placed the casserole dish back into the cabinet and began cleaning the puddle of melted ice on the floor.

The angels dissipated, returning to dust as I stood with my shoulders slumped in the hallway. While Mom wiped away the mess in the kitchen, I began to hope and pray for my father's return, for him to suddenly realize he could fix our broken family. I desperately prayed for God to intervene, to lock the doors of my father's truck, forcing him to do an about-face and saunter right back through the door of our gray house that had been so harshly slammed by my mother. I wanted God to forgive my father, and for my father to turn his shame into words and claim it was all a mistake: He was not leaving for California; he was not having an affair with his secretary; he did not mean to slam that casserole dish on Mom's head; it was all an accident, a momentary lapse, temporary insanity.

I rubbed at the wetness filling my eyes. Then I opened the front door to see if God had listened to my silent prayers. A summer day's glint turned our neighborhood into a mirage—a perfectly rotund cul-de-sac lined by houses with manicured hedges and rustic fences. My blinking eyes searched for my father's truck. It was parked in the street, fifty feet away from our front porch where I stood with my shoulders slumped. The engine was rumbling. I could see him through the rolled-up passenger window. He was smoking a cigarette, flicking ashes through a cracked window and onto the street. Our eyes met. Before I could call out or run to him, my father slowly eased the red Toyota single-cab away; tires crunched loose asphalt, metal gently rattled, ghostly hushes stirred among the still homes. I stood bewildered and blinking as my father disappeared among the ripples of glistening sunlight.

~

OVER THE NEXT FOUR YEARS, my father, Richard Kent Rand, became an apparition, a fleshless soul, a staticky voice from afar, rendered by phone or imagined in my dreams during the day and night. He materialized in my silent pleas to God. I asked God again and again to forgive him and the casserole dish incident, to be benevolent, not wrathful, and to return my father to his rightful home. Regrettably, my father did not return to our dusk-gray house because my pleas were heard. Instead, he returned to Corning, New York, with worn, red flesh under his eyes, because his first wife, his high school sweetheart, Anne, had died and his children were motherless.

~

ANNE'S CANCER HAD BEEN IN REMISSION when her husband of sixteen years left the family in 1980. She had been diagnosed with melanoma in the fall of 1971, when she was only twenty-six-years-old, a year after she gave birth to her third child. Biopsy after biopsy, surgery after surgery, her strong childbearing and childrearing body had become a patchwork of grafts and scar tissue. Healthy skin was taken from her legs and transplanted onto her maligned shoulders and stomach and lower back. She was unashamed of her body, wearing bikinis at public swimming pools, wounds exposed, her body a reminder that we all suffer.

~

SOON AFTER MY FATHER FLED Corning, New York, for San Jose, California, Mom's cancer returned with a vengeance. Numerous dark brown cancerous nodes were growing on her back and under the pit of one arm. Going to the confessional at Immaculate Heart of Mary raised her spirits, but it did not relieve her of immense physical pain. Faith soothed her soul, yet her body continued to decay like her favorite flower, primrose, at the end of her favorite season, fall.

After dinner one evening, Mom gathered us for a family meeting. These meetings were regular occurrences after my father departed. They became a new ritual, a potent mixture of raw emotions and gloomy forecasts, and by the end of each of these meetings I was often filled with numbness and dread. There was never a family meeting called to announce my sister's prowess on the tennis court or my brother's heroics on the baseball diamond or my budding jump shot. There was never any mention of slumber parties or summer camps or family vacations. Instead, we were told to tighten the budget (no new basketball shoes) or we had to change our behavior (no more fighting with fists) or we had to do more chores (actually pick up the dog's shit) or we argued about my father's worth. (Sadly, we often oscillated between tears and rage.) We were scared. We were worried. And, at times, we were desperate. A father, a husband, was thousands of miles away, and a mother, a wife, was sick.

We met in our spacious family room. Mom plopped down on our plaid couch. Kev and I sat next to her. Chris sat in a ratty brown recliner.

"I am going to have to have surgery again, but I need to do chemotherapy, too, which is medicine to make the cancer go away." She did not cry. She did not tremble. Her eyes were tranquil, not her usual fierce blue. Her voice was calm, not distant or frightful. Mom was as serene as a well-fed baby.

It was the first time I had heard the term *chemotherapy*. I had just turned twelve, and I immediately thought of the flavored liquid medicine a pediatrician, using a plastic syringe, squirts into your mouth when you are a child. This was also the first time my mother had ever *named* her illness in front of me. She had been battling cancer for a decade before saying the *word* in front of me. I am sure, had I joined her in a confessional, I would have heard her say the word *cancer*.

I was so used to hearing Mom say *I feel sick* instead of *I have cancer*, I became stupefied immediately instead of sad. Hearing technical terms, such as *chemotherapy* and *cancer*, made me think instead of feel, made me wonder instead of hurt, made me curious about how my mother's disease differed from the plagues recounted in the Bible or rabies that bats carried or muscular dystrophy, something discussed in our home each Labor Day, when my mother called and donated exactly two dollars each year after watching the comedic actor Jerry Lewis tell jokes and sing during an annual telethon.

"The doctors think the chemotherapy will work, but if it

doesn't, I may have to consider other options," Mom said. "I am not sure how this is going to turn out, but I want to live my life. I want to be happy. Even if it is only for a short time." Then my mother turned to her side, lifted her blouse so her back was exposed, and asked something extraordinary. "Do you want to touch the *cancer*?"

"No!" Kev bolted out of the living room, down the hall, and through the front door.

Chris shook her head, remained in the brown recliner, and rubbed her tears vigorously against her cheeks, which were apple-red. She inhaled raggedly.

I sat next to my mother and looked at her lower back where there were two half-dollar-sized growths the color of roasted coffee beans.

"You can touch them." My mother held my hand gently, guiding it to the small of her bare back.

"Does it hurt?" I asked as I ran my index and middle fingers over her tumors.

"No, I don't feel a thing."

Even though I was unable to fathom how discolored and soft, spongy tissue could damage her body, I was fascinated by those two large moles on my mother's back. They were, in my twelve-year-old mind, hypnotic, watches on a chain, mysterious dreams, and witchery. There were no angels hovering near while I caressed Mom's cancer. Only demons.

~

My mother went to Roswell Park Comprehensive Cancer Center in Buffalo, New York, to have those two devilish, brown nodes on her back surgically removed and to start an intensive chemotherapy regimen. According to my mother, my brother and I were too rambunctious to be left alone for a month with our sister, who had enough to worry about with school and tennis. So my father's mother, Ruby Rand, who we affectionately called Gram, came to stay with us, sleeping in our mother's bed and baking the most sinful apple pies while my mother battled her disease alone, a hundred miles from our home. This was the first of many month-long visits Gram made to our gray house over the next four years.

Gram had been a widow for nearly a decade when she showed up at our house, driving a Chevy Nova the color of her perfectly baked pie crusts. I was in charge of hauling her large, light blue suitcase from the car, up the stairs, and to Mom's room. I learned quickly that half of that hard-shell suitcase contained over a dozen Harlequin romance novels and colorful spools of yarn with various knitting needles. When Gram was not swirling around the kitchen with a rolling pin in one hand and a can of Tab soda in the other or hauling laundry up and down stairs or vacuuming our thick rugs in our dining and living rooms or directing Kev or me to walk our part-beagle, part-basset-hound dog named Muffet, she sat, knitting a hat or a scarf or mittens for an hour. Then, after placing her knitting on the end table, Gram picked up one of her Harlequins, with a title such as *Forbidden* or *Fool's Paradise* or *Dangerous Marriage*, and read for an hour. Then she napped for an hour. All in the same chair next to an end table with knitting and books piled high.

Gram let me read her Harlequin novels, yet, at age twelve, I struggled to fully appreciate the *soap opera*, as Gram called it. "These characters can never quite find the kinda love like your grandfather and me had. He was a tough man, but he was always there for me, there for the family, a loyal man. I guess I like these books 'cause they make me feel special—I didn't have to worry about that *soap opera* stuff."

I never had the courage to ask Gram why my dad was not more like my grandfather, Stanwood, or what she thought of her youngest child leaving the woman he had married and the children he had fathered. But I did have the courage to ask Cathy Leiser out, or, more accurately, it was Cathy who possessed the courage while I merely dialed the phone. Our romance, a first for me, lasted about as long as it took Gram to knit a pair of mittens and a hat–roughly one week.

~

Cathy had short, bright-blonde hair, deep dimples, shiny braces, long lashes, and she smiled perpetually as if the world were only made of light. She was adorable, unashamedly so, and sat in the back row of sixth-grade history class while I sat in the front row. In the middle of class one wintery day, she passed a note to me with her phone number and a message; *call me*.

I smiled a wide, buck-tooth smile and touched my inflamed cheeks. I straightened my body, covered in gooseflesh, hoping to recompose myself at my desk and continue to take notes from the chalkboard. But Mary Jo, who sat right behind me, tapped me on the shoulder.

"What did it say?" she whispered.

"Nothing," I snapped curtly.

"Stephen, you know there is no talking during class unless you are called upon," my teacher said, standing in front of me.

I nodded, acknowledging my transgression. My face was an inferno.

"Go to the corner of the room, pick up those two dictionaries, and hold out your arms. Keep your arms up and a dictionary in the palm of each of your hands. If you cannot do this for more than fifteen minutes, I will send you to the principal's office for further discipline."

Like so many awkward boys, I was growing rapidly, and my shirts barely fit. I was wearing a long-sleeve blue oxford buttoned tightly to my chin when I spread my arms to hold the dictionaries. The cuffs of my shirt cut into my forearms, and the collar dug into my neck. My Adam's apple felt like a stone stuck in my throat every time I swallowed. I must have looked like a poor rendering of the crucifixion. Oddly, while I held the dictionaries like sacred scriptures, I did not feel humiliated by the punishment. I was more embarrassed by the note I had tucked under my history textbook before ambling to the corner of the classroom, where I stood for the remainder of the class, well beyond the fifteen minutes my teacher stipulated. Luckily, I did not mind some exercise during history class, and, luckily, Cathy and I had something to talk about when I called her that night.

"I can't believe she made you do that."

"Yeah, I know."

"That must've sucked?"

"Not really. I've had worse."

"Really, like what?"

"My mom used to send me to summer school run by nuns. I got my knuckles rapped all the time. That hurt much more than holding a couple of dictionaries during class."

For the rest of the week, Cathy and I talked for an hour by phone each evening, barely speaking between classes during the day. There were too many distractions at school—friends and gossip, stuck lockers, and my sudden shyness. We met at the local skating rink on Friday night for our first date, which was also my first date. We skated for hours. Cathy was far less sure of herself on the ice than I was, but she smiled radiantly while slowly sliding one skate in front of the other, holding my hand as we circled the rink to the boom of "Private Eyes," by Hall and Oates. I was smitten for the first time in my life, and I began to understand romance as a fearless yet jubilant smile, Cathy's smile.

In the following days, Cathy explained to me on the phone how I was too bashful at school.

"Why don't you talk to me at school like you talk to me on the phone?"

"You see, I have to wear this retainer, and it makes my jaw clench, and I can't speak."

"If you can take the retainer out to answer questions in history, you can take the thing out to talk to me," she responded. Then she broke off our budding romance a few days after our first and only date. I turned to my sister for advice.

"Steve, when you like someone, you talk to them. A woman needs to know that you like her and you appreciate her and you want to be around her. Geez!" My sister, who was friends with Cathy's older sister, Lisa, clearly thought my excuse was lame, too.

Every time my sister ended a sentence with a loud and incredulous *geez*, I felt self-conscious, moronic, as if I had missed an important lesson about romance on TV or at school or at Bible study on Saturdays. I wondered if my father missed some lesson about romance along the way or if he felt ashamed of his diffidence and silence like me; maybe this is why I started to read Harlequin romances. But I only felt empty and confused and extremely bored while reading Gram's books. That is why, against my mother's wishes, I secretly purchased horror novels by Stephen King with my paper route money. I stashed the books between my box spring and mattress; not even my brother knew I kept *Cujo* and *Christine* hidden under me while I slept.

~

A FEW WEEKS AFTER I FELL IN and out of love with Cathy Leiser, my sister told me of another harsh reality that had nothing to do with romance but did fill me full of horror. I was sitting at the kitchen table, filling out a worksheet for my First Aid Merit Badge, which I needed for my First Class rank in Boy Scouts. I felt confident I understood what to do if someone had a cut or a bruise or a broken bone, but I wasn't sure what to do if someone had a burn, so I asked my sister, a Girl Scout, who was in the kitchen, preparing dinner while Gram folded laundry upstairs. Our mother was a hundred miles away, recovering from surgery and receiving treatment for internal injuries that were a mystery to me.

"There is not much you can do except pour cold water over the burn and maybe take some aspirin. If you're Mom, you put Noxzema on the burn, but I am not sure that helps much."

When my sister said this, I recalled several times when I had developed water blisters on my freckly shoulders because they were horribly sunburned. My mother would lather Noxzema on my shoulders, which cooled my fair skin, if only for a minute or two. Some of the water blisters on my shoulders would burst at night when I turned or tossed in bed. I would wake to soaked sheets. If any blisters needing draining remained, my mother would stick a sewing needle into the fleshy bubbles, and cool water would trickle down my back harmlessly while my mother told me, *Be careful of the sun.*

"Chris, how did Mom get cancer?"

Since Mom was suddenly open about her illness, I thought the question was permissible. I even assumed the word *cancer* could be bandied about without reproach. We were so deeply entrenched in this disease as a family—a decade-long struggle—that I was astounded it never occurred to me to ask someone how it all started. Admittedly, I did not want to ask my mother this question for fear of rousing painful memories. Plus, I was still unsure of what was allowed to be openly deliberated in our family and what was meant for the confessional.

"Steve." My sister walked around the counter and cabinets to the kitchen table where she stood, looking at me oddly, hugging a large glass bowl with one arm while stirring a plastic spatula. "She got it from the sun. Mom used to put Crisco oil all over her body, sometimes baby oil all over her body when she was young, your age, my age, until she was an adult, until she discovered she had what is called melanoma."

As if I were in a deep trance, I began to imagine the sun as a demon that poisoned my mother, burning her flesh so badly on the outside that her veins and muscles were bubbling with blisters; her insides were an ugly array of charred tissue that only God had the power to heal.

~

My mother was a swimmer from a very young age. Her father, Charles Morrell, affectionately known as Bump, bought more than thirty acres of land along the Worcester Range in Vermont, with the intent of turning the property into a summer camp. He dug a large hole, covered it with asphalt, dammed a nearby brook, ran pipes down a hill, and gravity fed the deep, asphalt hole with water, a pool heated by the sun. Then Bump put a wooden dining cart and a wooden caboose, which he acquired from Central Vermont Railway, the company he worked for, on the property. The railroad company was going to burn the decommissioned dining cart and caboose. My grandfather offered to pay for them, but a station manager told Bump, *If you get a flatbed truck to haul them away, you can have them for free.*

My grandfather obtained a flatbed truck and carved out a small slice of paradise for his entire family, a summer camp that came to be known as *The Caboose*, only a five-minute drive or a fifteen-minute bike ride from the family home in Waterbury, Vermont, where my mother spent her entire life until she married my father. Years of swimming at *The Caboose* exposed my mother's skin to a corruptive sun. Then, while in high school, my mother spent her summers as a lifeguard at the community pool. She swam and swam and swam, with only a cap and a suit, her body lathered with oil while sunlight radiated on the very waters she was raised in.

~

My mother also loved to dance, so much so she was invited onto a local television show called *Dance Date*, a popular music program broadcast from a studio in Burlington, Vermont. It was an hour-long car ride past bucolic farms to get to the *Big City* of Burlington. The show aired every Saturday night from 1955 to 1968 and every weekday afternoon on the local radio station in Waterbury, WDEV. The broadcast was a spinoff of the highly popular, nationally syndicated television show in Los Angeles, *American Bandstand*, hosted by the iconic Dick Clark, who remained youthful throughout his thirty-three-year career, from 1956 to 1989.

When my mother went on television in the early sixties, her family was able to watch her dance from afar, miles away, thanks to this new technology that became ubiquitous across America. At the time, my mother's family was certainly entertained and awestruck while watching her dance on the television, but there were other evocative images disseminating throughout the nation that could not be ignored. My mother's family witnessed horrible violence thousands of miles away where young and old Americans who happened to be Black were being brutally suppressed by rubber bullets, water hoses, noxious gas, and dogs. My family had a reckoning and a political awakening. These scenes, coupled with their Catholic moralism, shaped their political ideologies into something much more cosmopolitan. As descendants of Irish and Italian immigrants, my family took the pledge seriously; *One Nation under God, indivisible, with liberty and justice for all.* They became equally engaged in the country's social movement as much as, in some instances more than, the small-town politics in Waterbury.

Ken Greene, along with Waterbury's very own Brian Harwood, hosted *Dance Date* for its entire run of twelve years as rock and roll swept the nation thanks to Elvis Presley. My mother was not immune to the allure of these provocative dances, such as the *jive* or *jitterbug* or *boogie woogie.* Teens from the small hamlets of Vermont appeared on the show, dancing to the latest and greatest hits, such as the "Da Do Run Run Run" by the Crystals or Chubby Checker's "Let's Twist" or "Wild One" by Bobby Rydell. I imagine my mother's broad shoulders swiveling like a gyroscope as she danced and danced and danced, smiling gaily for hours until the music broadcast halted. Her body was strong then and full of vigor.

~

Anne was born on December 18, 1944, a stormy Monday with snow blanketing Heaton Hospital in Montpelier, Vermont. While Anne announced her presence on this cold earth, the U.S. Pacific Fleet was sailing unwittingly into a typhoon, the Battle of the Bulge had just begun, and President Franklin Delano Roosevelt, suffering from an assortment of ailments and disease, was convalescing at Warm Springs, Georgia. FDR had visited the small hamlet of Waterbury, Vermont, once. It was on August 1, 1936, the same day Hitler opened the Olympics in Germany. FDR traveled by train to visit the Waterbury Dam built by the Civilian Conservation Corps, arriving on a stretch of Central Vermont Railway track managed by Bump, who held an arm of the frail-legged President of the United States while accompanying him from the train station's ramp to a waiting car. Bump was thrilled to hear from the president's lips that he had a tranquil ride all the way from Washington, D.C.

Bump, the oldest son of resourceful Italian immigrants, was a compassionate yet tough-minded man, who revered food, family, and the railroad as much as he worshiped the pope, possibly more so. Neither priest nor family member condemned Charles Morrell for his extra meals or extra hours and days and years of service to Central Vermont Railway. Like many children of immigrants, he simply wished to honor his parents' perilous journey by embracing his daily toil, which ensured that his own children had ample amounts of love, food, and faith, and that certain traditions—homemade wines, homemade bolognese sauces—were upheld while new customs, such as graduating from not only primary or secondary schools but from colleges, were engendered.

When his wife, Florence, spoke of labor pains while making breakfast and filling lunch boxes on the morning of December 18, 1944, Bump immediately slung a long wool coat over his broad body, fastened a wool fedora hat with a thin brim to his balding head, and began shoveling the driveway. Then he swept the snow from his 1942 Nash 600, which he had purchased because the backseat rest was removable and a stretcher carrying his fourteen-year-old daughter, Dorothy, slid snugly in from the trunk side. It was like a metal cocoon for young Dorothy, who spread her arms wide and free if need be. Bump fancied the Nash 600 even though it was mechanically unsound, popping out of gear at the most inopportune times, but he needed a comfortable transport for his daughter, who suffered from a bone disease that forced her to wear bulky, black cumbersome shoes on both feet and an uncomfortable metal brace on one leg, similar to FDR.

On the morning of December 18, 1944, Dorothy, excited

about the prospect of a baby brother or sister, begged her parents to stay home from school. Bump, easily charmed and persuaded by each of his daughters, relented, and, as he had done for the President of the United States, steadied his daughter as she clopped to the car using crutches. Then he helped Florence shuffle through the snow and wind and cold.

He steered the Nash south, toward Montpelier, toward Heaton Hospital, unfazed by the Nash's willingness to suddenly slip gears, which jolted Dorothy, whose head knocked against the front bench seat while her legs bounced in the trunk.

Florence requested a stop at her mother's house before going to the hospital. There, Bump ate a second breakfast as the ladies, Dorothy included, talked about everything but the baby about to be born, mainly the weather and war. Florence's mother, Lottie, was in good spirits, though, and so were her two sisters, Glady and Margaret. The three of them wished Florence well, kissed her flushed cheeks, and watched Bump lay Dorothy gently into the Nash 600. For a man with thick hands, he had a soft touch.

Once Florence was settled into a bed at the hospital, Bump took Dorothy to work with him. They drove around Montpelier—the Nash stuttering and yammering like an anxious child—checking various job sites where crews repaired railway tracks and ties. They stopped by the hospital after each errand, receiving updates, remaining calm, suppressing excitement, adopting a stoic posture as much as winter would allow. Bump and Dorothy left the hospital around noon to have lunch at the train station in Montpelier. They ate sandwiches from a lunchbox and drank warm milk from a thermos packed by Florence before she had packed her own bag for her two-week stay in the hospital.

After lunch, Bump worked while Dorothy sat quietly, imagining all the wonderful games she would play with her new sibling. Now that Dorothy's younger brother, Chuck, was nine years old and running around with friends from school, she and her two older sisters, Charlotte and Patricia, were no longer able to convince him to play "dress up" or coerce him to do silly things for their own entertainment. Dorothy was glad that her father had brought her along, glad that she did not have to go to school like Chuck and Patricia. Charlotte had already graduated from Waterbury High School, and when she was not busily studying to become a nurse, she wrote letters of encouragement to soldiers abroad, young men from Waterbury, her friends and neighbors. Dorothy had the pleasure of being the only person in her family with permission to read Charlotte's hope-filled, prayer-filled, coquettish letters before they were sent off to Europe.

Charlotte carefully crafted the letters so they lacked whimsy and romance. She did not want the young men of Waterbury yearning for her in ways that might cause a boy to run from a fight, or worse yet, go AWOL, so she endowed her missives with devotion and constant reminders that there was a woman thousands of miles away *thinking of you, Bob* or *Mac* or *Jack* or *Ray* or *Pete*, desiring a cup of coffee, or a drive-in movie, or *let's go dancing once you return safely*. Her letters, although genuinely sympathetic, were in part written to hopeful suitors, young men needing the image of a soft face and full lips before a grueling march or chaotic battle or desperate sleep.

A few months before Anne was born, Charlotte was forced to confront the powerful allure her letters produced. She was sitting on the front porch with her sisters and mother. They were talking about the weather and war, snapping the ends off stringy green beans and admiring the beauty of fall in Vermont when Pete Martin, on leave from the Air Force and wearing a crisp blue uniform, ambled up onto the red brick porch. Greetings were exchanged. Then Pete, with military perfunctory, knelt on one knee before Charlotte, and, in front of Charlotte's sisters and mother, pulled a dazzling ring from his pocket and proposed. "Before I ship out, we ought to get married."

It was difficult to ascertain how long Charlotte's radiant eyes held excitement or how broad her rapt smile might have grown as she gawked at the ring just placed on her finger, because Florence, looking up from the bowl of string beans, said, rather plainly, "You need to give that ring back to Pete." Florence kept shucking beans. Dorothy and Patricia kept their eyes on their older sister, who simply nodded at her mother as if she was just asked to do a simple chore.

"Pete, how about we go for a walk around the river?" Charlotte said, knowing it was not a question but an exit strategy. Pete complied.

Florence knew that a *walk around the river* was what lovers who lived in Waterbury did: strolling on the dirt roads rimming the Winooski River at dusk, ducking behind trees to make out, and stretching that river walk into a romantic odyssey before reaching the bridge that thrust young lovers back onto the dullness of Main Street. And Florence knew that Charlotte had taken many walks around the river as a teenager, and only a few of those had been with Pete.

Charlotte eventually returned to the house without Pete and without the ring. The engagement had lasted for approximately one hour.

~

My father, Richard, was working in Upstate New York when he proposed to my mother in 1963. My grandmother, Florence, did not intervene as she did with Charlotte's engagement. She knew her youngest child was ready to settle down and start a family even though her daughter had recently graduated from high school and had seen very little of the world outside of Waterbury. Plus, as was the custom that seemingly eluded Pete Martin on a fall day in 1944, my father had the wherewithal to ask my mother's parents for their permission and blessings to marry his longtime girlfriend. Father Logue of Saint Andrews Parish, a cherished friend of the family, performed the ceremony in the summer of 1964, sanctifying the union between two high school sweethearts.

My mother was a sophomore and my father was a senior at Waterbury High School when they first met. Richard had just moved to town from Maine. He was a charming teenager, quick-witted, knowledgeable about cars, and a decent basketball player. During games, Anne danced around the gym with all the other cheerleaders, her genuine and brilliant smile penetrating the must and chill of the low-lit gym. She enjoyed her friendships much more than the cheering and the score of the game, and so did Richard. They were an amiable couple.

~

DURING HER SENIOR YEAR, Anne was crowned prom queen and Steve Anderson was the king. Dick had graduated in 1961 and immediately took a job out of high school building roads for Lane Construction Company. He was hired as an accountant and relocated to a field office in Upstate New York. He drove several hours to attend and accompany my mother to the prom. This gesture solidified Anne's belief that she would be in New York soon enough. Graduation was only a few weeks away.

The theme of the prom that evening of May 24, 1963, was *Drifting and Dreaming*. The gymnasium was transformed into celestial scenes of a sky and a sea. Voluminous clouds hung beneath a blue netting with many silver stars and moons. The bandstand was framed in a black background with artificial grass in the foreground. There were pastel-colored tissue flowers and a lighted pool for ambiance.

Anne sat in a large basket chair with a crown covering her short brown hair. Blue lights produced the effect of rippling water at her feet. Overhead, white lights billowed like clouds moving quickly in the nighttime. Yellow sailboats were anchored nearby Anne. The heavens may have drifted into her mind. But doubtful. It was more likely she dreamt of her sweetheart, Dick, and a life beyond Waterbury, Vermont, or maybe she was thinking of her friends, one of whom had written a prophetic message to Anne on the back of her senior photo. She wrote, *Anne, you've got the looks, personality, and the know-how to get a boy, but they can be dangerous!*

~

MY FATHER'S FIRST EXTRAMARITAL AFFAIR was in 1969, five years after the wedding. We were living in Oswego, New York. My sister was a freckly-faced four-year-old, and I was about to have my first birthday. Our family lived in a small, white mobile home among many white mobile homes near Lake Ontario. My father was slowly rising through the ranks as an office manager for Lane Construction while my mother tended to the trailer, my sister, and me. Although the winter winds from the lake made trailer life harsh and bitter for months on end, my parents were content and happy. They knew we would be moving from one mobile home to the next as construction crews laid gravel and asphalt, as bridges and highways were fashioned into cold, hard arteries across America thanks to Eisenhower's dream of interstate travel.

Like his father, Stanwood, my father was willing to go to where the work was, even if it meant uprooting the family every two or three years. Once the roads were paved, the

Prom 1963

work moved hundreds of miles west or south or north or east. Predictable and plentiful, the work fed those families willing to follow the machinery through the country's labyrinths. My father, since he had lived an uprooted life as a child, presumed his wife, who attended the same school from first grade until graduation and who lived in the same home her entire life until marriage, would adapt while his children would be no worse for the wear. A home was ephemeral in my father's mind, merely a place to store food and to sleep, an icebox, a bunkhouse, an impermanent fixture that could easily be replaced like engine oil, like worn tires.

My father had an affair with the wife of a boyhood friend in 1969. Word of my father's infidelity had spread through the small-town channels of Waterbury, finding its way to my mother, who immediately packed her bags, my sister, and me, a chubby baby less than a year old, and left the white mobile home in Oswego. According to her sisters, my mother confronted my father before leaving. He claimed, "She needed me to comfort her because her husband was treating her terribly."

My mother returned to her childhood home, where Chris and I were properly doted on by our grandparents, Charles and Florence, Bump and Nanny. They knew nothing of my father's tryst. My mother told them we would be visiting for several weeks and left it at that. But her older sisters knew of the affair so when it came time to return to Oswego, they asked, "Why are you going?"

"I love him, and I want to make this work," my mother responded.

The fallout from the affair was immense. My father lost a friend from childhood, whose fragile marriage quickly collapsed. The wife suffered terribly. She fled Waterbury, fled the United States; shame drove her to become a missionary abroad. She proselytized about Heaven, about sin, and about transgressions of the flesh. She continued this work for more than fifty years. As for my mother, she refused to divorce my father, reconsecrated the marriage, discovered she was pregnant with my baby brother, and, less than a year after Kev was born, learned she had melanoma.

Immediately after my mother's diagnosis, bits of her body were removed; cancerous chunks of flesh were taken from her shoulders and stomach while her heart was painfully breaking from a tenuous marriage to a man who refused to admit that he did anything wrong, declaring that he was only guilty of easing a woman's suffering as if she were a child with a splinter or a bird with a broken wing. The harder my mother worked at the marriage, the more stubborn and withdrawn my father became. He slowly stopped attending church, wholly and quietly disappeared into his work, and stole money from his employer.

~

IN 1971, MY MOTHER'S PROGNOSIS was not great, but it was not hopeless. The doctors felt confident they had removed all the diseased tissue, though the probability of her cancer returning was high. Of course, I knew none of this at the time. When my father brought the three of us to the hospital to visit our mother, Chris, Kev, and I were told, *Your mother is sick, but she is feeling better.* Shortly after that visit, the three of us were told, *We are moving.* Luckily, we were not traveling abroad, chasing after a mistress full of shame. We were heading south, below the Mason-Dixon Line.

~

WE MOVED FROM OSWEGO, NEW YORK, to Washington, D.C., during the summer of '72. My father was able to find a job as an office manager even though he had been fired from Lane Construction because he was caught embezzling money. He had been taking money from the petty cash drawer at his office. For what purpose, my mother never discovered. She rifled through his pant pockets, blazer pockets, winter coat, shoe-shine box, shaving kit bag, and the glove compartment of the family station wagon. Receipts never materialized, yet checks bounced and bills went unpaid. My father did not drink, he did not gamble, and he did not go to jail for pilfering the petty cash drawer because his boss pitied him, pitied a man with an ill wife and three young children. My father's boss simply asked my father to pay back the stolen money, then he told him to find a different place to work, but not before my father pawned my mother's diamond ring to settle his debt. According to her sister-in-law, my mother confronted my father about the ring, a family heirloom. He denied knowing its whereabouts.

Money seemed to appear then vanish as if it were a mirage, yet my mother stuck by her man, a man she had fallen in love with as an effervescent sixteen-year-old girl, a man she hoped would stop being dishonest and return to being the charming basketball player who made her laugh. Not cry. She placed enormous hope in my father. She asked him to remain faithful, to remain by her side if her cancer returned, and to show two boys how to become men.

Luckily, my father cobbled together enough money to purchase a single-story, blonde-brick home in a suburb of D.C. Directly across from our new home was a large playground nestled in a wooded area where my brother and I constantly fell from a towering jungle gym. Much like our family life, the playground offered tremendous pain and pleasure. Mom became an ad hoc nurse with little compassion after we moved into our new home. *If you boys crack your skulls open, don't come running to me*—which she said often while cleaning skinned knees or treating bloody noses or icing swollen eyes from our ruckus play.

On any given day, Kev or I had a battered body that needed mending, and my mother was quick to reprimand but even quicker to remind us; *It may hurt now, but the pain will go away. It lasts as long as or as little as you want it to.* My father used fewer words to express similar sentiment; *Suck it up.* These words, as they were repeated throughout our childhood, became our mantras, leading my brother and me to have little, if any, concern for what happened to our bodies. We became increasingly reckless in fields of play as we hardened with age.

While we lived in the District of Columbia, my parents were able to salvage some semblance of a marriage, if only in appearance, after creating sufficient distance from their problems and separating themselves from scandalous temptations, life-threatening surgeries, embezzlement, and deceit. I sensed, even though I only rose to the height of my mother's waist, no disharmony in their marriage, nor, I suspect, did their many friends and family members who passed through our front door—a glass door I once ran through while chasing my brother (the scars on my body from this incident were demure in size and texture as compared to my mother's).

My father charmed everyone into believing he was a devoted husband and father, convincing family, friends, acquaintances, and himself that our family was a portrait of America's wholesomeness, god-fearing-yet-proud-of-our-daily-toil family. It was as if my father sketched our family into a Norman Rockwell painting alongside all of its endearments and idealism and whiteness. We became bound to this myth, a profound story of a family accepting a predetermined fate: backyard barbecues, big cars, football games, toy muskets, Boy and Girl Scouts, catechism, and Walt Disney World. As witless as our acceptance was of this illusionary lifestyle, it offered comfort, a temporary amelioration of our woes, which is why my mother was complicit in this Rockwellian ruse.

~

"Has everyone gone to the bathroom?" my mother asked after we piled into the car. "We are not stopping for a while."

Kev, Chris, and I offered faint *yeses* as my father put the white Oldsmobile station wagon with faux woodgrain trim into reverse and backed us out of the driveway. The sun was still rising over our blonde-brick home in the nation's capital. My father looked into the rearview mirror. Kev, Chris, and I sat in the wide backseat. Our mother, wearing bug-eyed sunglasses, sat in the front seat. Her feathery dark hair rested on her shoulders, curled and thoroughly combed as if she had been up for hours preparing before the long journey to Florida.

"Space Mountain just opened a few months ago," my father said, smiling into the rearview mirror. "It oughta be a heck of a ride." He loved rollercoasters.

By the time the Oldsmobile eased onto one of Eisenhower's interstates, heading south toward Walt Disney World, Kev and I were fully awake and playing in the way back of the station wagon. All of our luggage was in a canvas bag tied to the roof rack, so Kev and I had plenty of room to turn the rear of the car into a wrestling ring. If we bent our knees and waist, we were able to stand. The wagon bound down the highway, and I began to slam my six-year-old body into Kev's four-year-old body playfully. Then I pinned his shoulders and pretended to be a referee delivering a three count, slapping my palm on the floor; *tum, tum, tum.*

"What is going on back there?" my mother roared.

Kev pushed me off. We concealed our bodies behind the backseat, giggling then *shushing* each other.

"Boys, there will be no horsing around in the back," my mother said. "Why don't you grab the crayons and coloring books I got you."

Kev and I spread our bodies in the way back of the wagon and commenced to coloring Disney cartoon characters. For hours, I fought to keep the colors within the outlines of Goofy and Pluto and Donald Duck as the car bounced on the interstate. Glancing out of the rear window at the unfamiliar scenes, I felt as if I were viewing the world through a stereoscope. The trees and sky rushed by like a slideshow, and when I blinked, the slides advanced. The white Oldsmobile station wagon had become a child's toy, a giant View-Master advancing a reel of America. I desperately tried not to blink, not to advance the slide as the world hurried by, but my eyes became dry and my eyelids flickered like dying light.

As dusk approached, my father pulled the giant View-Master into the parking lot of a colorful motel next to the highway. We helped our father unpack the suitcases and waited for him to change into his bathing suit. Once he tied the waistband and slid into his sandals, Chris, Kev, and I sprinted to the pool, where many families splashed around in the water or sat in lounge chairs, chatting boisterously. After a long day of driving, my father, with a slight paunch hanging over tight white shorts, paced around the pool, smoking Marlboro cigarettes, flicking ashes to the ground, and striking up conversations with strangers. Periodically, he peeked at us, ensuring Kev and I stayed in the shallow end because neither of us could swim, acting as our lifeguard while my mother relaxed in a chair, still wearing her bug-eyed sunglasses even though the sun was disappearing. Just as the last light of day remained over Florida, my father strolled onto the diving board, took two large steps then one short step while raising one knee much higher than the other, bounced high off the board and into the air, turned his body into a plank, and landed in the water, barely creating a splash. A meticulous dive under the deep orange sky. He swam the length of the pool underwater to get to the three of us, rising from the deep, lifting us, tossing us, tickling us, telling us how grand Space Mountain was going to be, how we needed to prepare for the most spectacular rollercoaster in the world.

We rose early the next morning, dressed and ate breakfast excitedly. A half an hour later, my father steered the Oldsmobile into an enormous parking lot. It was quiet and hazy. We walked past many empty station wagons before hopping into a white monorail cab with red streaks heading to the Magic Kingdom. We had the cab to ourselves as the train snaked methodically over an expansive swath of well-groomed, deep green fields before crossing a narrow river and stopping in front of the entrance to a pristine world full of spectacle. The haze of the day suddenly disappeared.

As we entered the Magic Kingdom, we were greeted by Mickey and Minnie Mouse, both standing on a veranda about twice my height. Two large mice were dressed in formal attire. They were waving to hundreds of fixed smiles huddled around the tall veranda as ebullient music blared in the streets. Adults and children wore shirts or hats with images of Minnie or Mickey. By the end of our first day at Disney World, my parents had purchased a white hat with Minnie striking a pose for my sister and a white T-shirt with Mickey's large smiling face draped across the front for me. The next day, my parents purchased black tricorn hats and toy muskets for Kev and me. The hat barely rested on my towhead, but it kept a blistering sun from my eyes on the third day when we toured Adventureland, Frontierland, and Tomorrowland.

I was nervous as I shuffled to the measuring station at the entrance of Space Mountain, Tomorrowland's main attraction.

Kevin (left), Chris (center), Steve (right)

My sister kept telling me there was a height requirement while my father and mother kept telling me not to worry about it, that I was tall enough. As I stepped under a *You Must Be This Tall* sign, I removed my tricorn hat, inhaled deeply, and straightened my back. I looked up at my parents. They smiled. I thrust my tricorn hat into my mother's hands, turned, and sprinted inside the large dome encasing the rollercoaster. My father yelled, "Wait for your sister and me!"

The clicking chain of the four-seat coaster car shaped like a rocket made my head buzz as it climbed the track. Everything was dark, except for the soft lit stars in the space-scape scenery above. I was only six. And climbing to the heavens. Aside from some clicks and thumps, the universe appeared still with slight flickers of light. My father sat in the seat behind me. He asked, "Are you ready for this? Here we go."

Before I could answer, we plunged down into the dark sea of space, twisting and turning like frightened snakes. We were on a train steaming toward the stars, touring the universe, unable to see the track before us, astonished when our direction changed radically. We had no control. And the suddenness of changing directions without warning was exhilarating. Frightful.

When Walt Disney World opened in 1971, Bump was asked to help maintain the resort's monorail system. He turned down the job offer, not wanting to uproot his wife and daughter, Dorothy, or leave his siblings and in-laws, or miss any of the excitement involving his twelve grandchildren. He had planted his roots firmly, unlike his youngest daughter, who sat with her youngest child outside of Space Mountain, holding hats of the revolution, eating ice cream, waiting patiently for her husband and two children to finish the thrilling rollercoaster ride. This Magic Kingdom was not the one she dreamt of.

~

AT THE PEAK OF EVERY SUMMER, my mother dutifully herded her family into a Sears Portrait Studio as if we were livestock going to market, parading our perfectly even bangs—thanks to our father's meticulous nature with scissors, combs, and electric clippers. Before the photo shoot commenced, my mother scoured the children's clothing racks for bargains in the Sears department store. During these manic hunts for outfits, my mother would quip, "You are going to have clean clothes for these pictures, no stains, no rips, nothing soiled."

Once these items were purchased, my mother would tear the price tags off and shoo us into dressing rooms. We were transformed into sanitized versions of ourselves. Our scabs were covered, bruises obscured, rogue hairs combed into submission. We were far too young and ignorant to understand our mother's dream of a pristine family and her need to have us sit for portraits without blemishes, without scars, without betrayals.

My mother liked to have my brother and me wear matching outfits as if we were identical twins. My sister was grateful to not be forced to wear anything similar to her heedless brothers. In our first portrait as a family, my brother and I wore plaid polyester pants, solid brown turtlenecks, and thick-soled, burnt brown Hush Puppy shoes. It was always easy for me to smile, which was not the case for my brother. There were times when he was obstinate, refusing to smile during these choreographed photo shoots, acting as if the world was without humor or light. When this happened, patient photographers prodded, modeling the cheeriest of smiles then, inevitably, coerced a smile by placing a sweet treat in my brother's hands. When Kev was obstinate, my mother remained calm and encouraging throughout these sittings while my father scowled at his son's defiance.

One of the earliest portraits became a Christmas card sent

to family and friends in 1973. My brother and I wore tight white shorts and matching white sweater vests with small, embroidered tennis rackets on our chests as if we were somehow affiliated with a country club. Yes, my sister would become a talented tennis player, but she never played matches at a country club. Certain realities were absent from the portrait. For instance, the foreground of this portrait was bright blue while the background was the color of smoke in a cloudy sky. There was a cheeriness in our toothy smiles, even in the midst of the cloudy gray backdrop. Our mother's smile off camera brought out the best of us, and we were too young to feign anything other than our giggling hearts. I suppose in some instances, such as this portrait, my father may have been charmed by my mother's smile and her ability to express genuine joy. But then again, he was not smiling much in those days, possibly from shame, more likely from his severe gingivitis. His teeth were rotting, and it showed in the portraits.

My mother was extremely conscientious about our teeth. She had perfectly aligned rows of glistening teeth, two strings of pearls, while my father, neglecting his own diseased flesh, wore dentures. He contracted a severe case of gingivitis when he was thirty, losing a tooth here and there until my mother demanded he seek out an oral surgeon. He was having trouble eating, complaining for months, only to succumb to my mother's insistence, returning home from the hospital toothless, in pain, whining about how he could only slurp soup. After several weeks, he had pristine fake teeth, complaining only when he had iced tea with soup; the chill and heat caused him headaches.

This ritual of immortalizing resplendent and wholesome portraits, with their pristine clothes wrenched from racks, created a pretense that lasted over eight arduous years—from the time my brother turned two years old up until he joined my Little League Baseball team. Clearly, our parents perpetuated

Front row: Dick, Anne, Kev; back row: Chris and Steve

the myth of a family *unbroken* until the fate-filled day when my father slammed a casserole dish on my mother's skull.

It was shortly after the divorce when my mother's family cut my father out of all the portraits that were hanging on the living room walls, choosing instead to remember only Anne's brilliant smile and her children's benign bliss. The family never knew about the casserole dish.

~

THE YEAR OF THE BICENTENNIAL commemorating the Declaration of Independence and the subsequent American Revolution was an exciting time to be in Washington D.C. The celebration stirred many sentiments of America's distant past, yet, at seven years old, it did not feel so distant to me. Instead, the pageantry engrossing the city made it seem as if America's break from England was merely a few short years removed instead of two hundred.

I was captivated by history in school, often reading from boxes full of large, laminated cards in my second-grade classroom. These boxes were considered reading laboratories. Each laminated card had illustrations on the front and back with thick paragraph descriptions. The entire Revolutionary War was conveyed in only a few paragraphs, from Paul Revere's historic ride to Cornwallis's surrender at Yorktown. Usually, I lost track of time while reading from these boxes, consuming history as if it were a drama unfolding with each word, each sentence. There were many instances when my imagination got the best of me, and I began to travel in time, transporting myself to places like Boston or Philadelphia in 1776, embracing the romance of revolution. I fell in and out of love with so many people and so many places from the past. Consequently, the peril of death on a battlefield was the glory I imagined and sought as a foolish child.

In 1976, the nostalgic scenes of the American Revolutionary War played out in our streets. Many men of all ages marched in parades, wearing uniforms of the revolution: blue wool jackets, white breeches, white stockings, and tricorn hats. They carried antique muskets while they proudly marched in unison as iconic patriots along the streets of downtown D.C. Women wore bonnets and walked with children waving miniature American flags with thirteen stars for each colony, conjuring the tale of Betsy Ross and a mythical origin story of the birth of a grand nation.

On this special fourth of July, I tucked my mended jeans, with iron-on patches, into long, white tube socks, fixed my tricorn hat from Walt Disney World, and slung my toy musket over my shoulder. I completely transformed into a soldier of the revolution and paraded about the neighborhood as if I were a war hero fighting at Valley Forge or Ticonderoga. Charming neighbors waved flags as fireworks erupted on manicured lawns. How wholesome suburban families appeared under the sun, casting shadows from the past while illuminating the present.

How I fell in love with revolutionary uniforms; how I fell in love with America; how I fell deeply in love with the concept of glory and sacrifice, words I had heard many times during church. But these scenes were different from anything else I had ever encountered. These images of defying an empire felt miraculous. Overcoming tyranny (a word I did not fully understand at age seven) felt powerful, energizing, so much more so than the words I recited or heard or read while attending church or Bible study.

~

DURING THE SUMMER OF 1976, my cousin Jane took a train to Washington D.C. She had recently graduated from the University of Vermont. My parents asked her to babysit while they searched for a house in Corning, New York, east of Buffalo and near the northern border of Pennsylvania. My father was leaving the security of Eisenhower's thruways for the damming of an old waterway, the Tioga River, a tributary of the Susquehanna River. It was one of the oldest rivers in the world, older than the mountains surrounding it. Two separate dams needed to be built; one along the Tioga River, a few miles beyond the border of Pennsylvania, and another dam farther south, near Pittsburgh at a place called Crooked Creek.

When my cousin Jane arrived at our house, my mother most likely provided explicit advice to her niece: *Try to keep the boys from fighting and make sure they do their chores.* Shortly after my parents left for New York, Jane asked me to clean my room. I went into my bedroom, opened a window, and climbed out, promptly exiting my room. We lived in a one-story house, so the drop from the window was about as tall as a midsummer cornstalk. Luckily, my seven-year-old body was as pliable as a Gumby doll. I contorted my body and landed on my feet easily enough. I had done this dance many times before.

I quickly ran across the street to the wooded park, a refuge where I often scurried to the top of a jungle gym and hung upside down like a bat, securing the bridge of both my feet under a metal bar, laying the back of my thighs on an adjacent bar, lowering my torso, and folding my arms together like an X. I enjoyed rocking back and forth while upside down, although my scalp would start to tingle as I watched the shadows of my body cast on the ground below. Eventually, blood would rush to my head while I swayed, watching my shadowy self as the world remained topsy turvy. Dangling like a bat was exhilarating, reshaping my perspective, forcing me to see different realities.

When I heedlessly escaped through my bedroom window, only to shirk my responsibilities, I was, in effect, embracing the ambiguity of child's play, mixing the harsh realities of responsibility and a pretend world where I was a revolutionary patriot fighting against tyrannical redcoats, imagining defiance of authorities. I was unaware of these vague notions resembling boundaries to be tested. My cousin, Jane, who was only doing the bidding of my mother, looked out of the window and saw me running wildly to the park across the street. She may have laughed or cursed or simply thought, *What a brat.*

I never fully understood why I ran. It just seemed to be a natural inclination, as if I had to simply disappear like a ghost. I did this often in my youth, vanishing from home or school but never church or the soccer field. Freedom to move about on a whim, defying the authorities—namely my mother and babysitters—were frivolous luxuries until my body required repair.

~

It was a gray, late-fall day when I started climbing the jungle gym at the elementary school in Bowie, Maryland. When I arrived at the top of the play structure, I sat and swung my legs, fidgeting like so many seven-year-olds desiring an adventure. I had the jungle gym to myself. My classmates seemed distant, seesawing, swinging, or rushing down the slide. I turned my head and looked around. The woods behind me were filled with trees dropping leaves, and the forest ended where a flat field began. I quickly climbed down the jungle gym and ran toward a chain link fence at the point where the forest met the field. As I approached the fence, I picked up my pace, pumping my arms in a sprinter-like fashion. Then I leapt at the fence, clutching the links, and scurried like a squirrel to the top of the six-foot metal fence.

When I reached the top, I swung my left leg over the fence. Then I swung my right leg. My brand-new brown corduroy pant leg got caught on a metal link and ripped from the crotch to the bellbottom. Blood began trickling down my right leg as I dangled and held onto the top of the fence. I was scared and hurting. My left hand was sweaty and slipped. It caught on a sharp piece of the metal fence as I fell, landing on my back. I got up immediately and looked at my left hand. My pinky was throbbing and bleeding. I began to cry profusely, running gingerly the length of the fence, past my classmates, and into the front office of the school.

When my mother walked into the school nurse's office, her eyes widened, searching my body for damage, determining whether I was broken or unbroken. "My God, what did you do, Stephen?"

I shrugged my slouching shoulders. Then I tried to cover up my crotch with pieces of my corduroy pant leg because my underwear was visible to all.

"He has a deep cut in his pinky. I bandaged it. He will need stitches." the nurse said. "His leg is fine. I cleaned up his scratches."

"Thank you," my mother said. Then she grabbed my undamaged forearm and jerked my slouching body out of the chair, pulling me through the hallway while I tried to cover my crotch with my bandaged hand.

My mother hurried us to the car. I galloped alongside her, favoring my right leg as she pulled me along by the forearm. Then she shooed me into the car like I was a stray dog.

"I can't believe you! You ruined your school pants! I am not buying another pair. I hope you learned a lesson. I don't want any more climbing fences. What were you thinking, Stephen?"

When she was upset with me, my mother always called

me *Stephen* instead of *Steve*, making me feel ashamed when I heard my full given name. My response was always a shrug of my slouching shoulders.

As my mother pulled into the doctor's office, I was thinking I had no earthly idea why I'd climbed the fence. It was there, ready to climb, and I'd wanted to disappear and run from whatever it was that had compelled me to run in the first place.

In the waiting room, my mother remained silent until we were called to the exam room. Then she turned to me and said, "It may hurt now, but the pain will go away. It lasts as long as or as little as you want it to." She was raised by parents of the depression, and her own body was a patchwork of scars. I could not help but feel foolish as well as ashamed.

The doctor realized I was having trouble sitting still while he examined my finger, so he allowed me to stand. Plus, I was short enough I did not have to stoop, only slouch slightly as my elbow and hand rested on a countertop. My mom held my left hand firmly while the doctor cleaned my wound and stitched my pinky. It was a deep cut with no significant damage. He claimed I would live to climb another day. Prodigious tears fell from my lashes as I rubbed my eyes raw with my good hand. I was trying not to shake or cry or take off running. Instead, I looked at my mother. She was focused on my wound, asking the doctor questions about the healing process and how to care for her son.

Three prickly stitches were all I needed. My hand tingled for a week. Then, after another week, my mother took me back to the doctor's office to have the stitches removed. On the ride home I admired my scar, because it was the most painful injury I had suffered up until that point of time in my short life. But the damage to my body was my own doing, something I could have controlled, yet I was a typical, impetuous child unable to comprehend his actions. It was a pain unlike my mother's, whose scars were formed from injuries hidden inside her body, a body she had little control over.

~

My grandparents and aunts and uncles and cousins frequently traveled by train or plane from Vermont or Maine to Washington D.C. They enjoyed the ride on the plane or train as much as, possibly even more than, the many historical sites and the clamor of a big city. During their many visits, we would always tour the National Mall, which I never tired of, relishing the wonderment found inside the national monuments and Smithsonian museums. The National Museum of Natural History and the National Air and Space Museum were my favorites. I was mesmerized by the life-like installations of a Neanderthal family gathered around a fire or the stuffed monkey, Able, who sat in a capsule like the one that rocketed into orbit in 1959. Able wore an orange spacesuit, and his brown body hair jutted from his white helmet and the cuffs of his suit. I liked to run frenetically, holding one of my cousin's or aunt's or my mother's hand, pulling them close to the many different exhibits. I would prattle on about what I saw.

"How did the monkey eat while in space? His hands are strapped to his seat. How did he steer the spaceship? He is so small. He must've been cramped. Do you think he liked space? I wanna be an astronaut and go into space with a monkey. Someone like Curious George…"

~

My mother enjoyed bringing us to the public library near our house in Bowie, Maryland. An adventure that overwhelmed the senses. Musty curtains and creaky floors led to aisles of monolithic bookshelves filled with colorful covers and titles such as *The Giant Jam Sandwich, Rikki-Tikki-Tavi, Lowly Worm's Applecar*, inventive stories that stimulated my imagination in ways I have never recovered from. My world became dramatic and mystical when we visited the library. At the time, I did not understand the arc of storytelling, and how intuitive it is for many children. I only knew I wanted to be part of the stories—particularly, stories of good overcoming evil.

My sister, brother, and I would often check out the maximum number of books. We would cradle these adventures with both arms tight to our chest as we skipped to the car. Once we arrived home, we would lay our books out on our family room rug and begin to read for the remainder of the day and into the evening. Sometimes we exchanged books as we finished them. My sister's stack was more advanced, pages without illustrations. But I tried to comprehend the stories, asking my sister to help me pronounce unfamiliar words. It did not take long before my concentration waned while trying to read books by Judy Blume. Like many children playing with language at a young age, I decided to make the story up while pretending to read each word. New worlds were discovered while I read.

I liked to lie prone with my chin resting on my palms steadily. Then I would swing my calves like scissors, back and forth, cutting into the humidity for hours as my thighs rested on the soft shagginess of the ivory-colored carpet. Sometimes I used my index finger to track words as I read. Usually, I concentrated on imagining characters and worlds beyond the page, a swarm of bees lifting a jam sandwich, talking mongooses and snakes, worms that drive and wear bowties, all of whom embark on grand adventures of good versus evil. The musty, creaky, artistry aesthetic of libraries were (and continue to be) my salvation, my sanctuary.

I began kindergarten in 1973. My first ever assignment for

school was to research an animal and share what I learned with the class. With my shoulders slumped and my beaver-like teeth protruding, I marched with my class single file to the library where there were several tables full of picture books about animals. I quickly grabbed a book with an enormous bat on the cover. It had many, many photographs to aid my research. I sat, started reading, and quickly learned bats had hair. My five-year-old mind struggled to understand how these creatures could fly like birds without feathers. Then I read about how bats were *mammals*, a word that confused me, so I read more, and I discovered their vision was limited, so they needed the aid of sounds (*sonar*) to fly at night. These discoveries opened an entire world of wonderment for me, so much so that school became another sanctuary beyond the public library, the Catholic Church, and fields of play.

I showed my mother the book about bats as soon as I got home from school, splaying it out on the kitchen table like a freshly dressed fish. Then I began prattling on about everything I had learned, pointing to pictures, explaining my discoveries, asking about this curious word *mammal*.

"Well, we are *mammals*. We have hair because we descended from apes."

"*Descended?*"

"We were once apes."

"You mean like *Planet of the Apes?*"

"Yes, much like *Planet of the Apes*."

I was so flummoxed by my mother's words, it took years to reconcile the contradiction between *The Planet of the Apes* and the Garden of Eden. My confusion lasted a long time, because I fervently believed that everyone on the planet had descended from Adam and Eve. I just assumed, ignorantly, that the Neanderthals in the Smithsonian National Museum of Natural History were begotten by Adam and Eve. Eventually, I encountered a biology class that disabused me of the Bible's creation myth—a truly awful trick of the mind, having to imagine an archaic cave instead of a fruitful garden. This was the most disappointing revelation because Eden was colorful while evolution was a gray, cold stone. Unfortunately, it was too late to ask my mother more questions about faith or biology. She was a hundred miles away receiving treatment. I did not have the heart to ask Gram. I did not want to upset her with talk of evolution. My father was three thousand miles away, rarely calling, so it seemed to me that he had fewer and fewer answers regarding the origins of humanity or the reasons for my existence or any ideas about his own existence. It was as if my father had crawled into a cave and curled up like an amoeba, living a life filled with pathos.

~

DURING ALL THE TIMES we toured the Smithsonian museums and the Mall monuments with family visiting from Vermont or Maine, my father tended to be absent, often working, avoiding his in-laws. He acted cordial around his own family, half-smiling during dinners. Conversely, my mother held wide smiles during dinner. She laughed with ease, a gracious hostess, still young, only in her twenties, and full of vitality even after the cancer diagnosis. My father's family adored my mother, which made gatherings awkward for my father, whose shame may have compelled him to keep his hands and mind busy by meticulously cleaning.

I watched my father with fascination after dinners when he would painstakingly scrape food off plates as if whittling clay with a metal fork tine, every crumb or drop of gravy flung firmly into the garbage can. Then he would vigorously scrub and closely inspect each plate before rinsing. He would wipe plates and glasses and silverware with both hands holding one towel, buffing and polishing each item as if it were a jewel or a leather shoe. Then he would place everything back into the cabinets or drawers carefully without a bare finger touching the sanitized items. He did all of this while whistling or humming, as if everything was in order. When he cleaned, any shame he possessed seemed to wash away with the debris and dust, as if the act of cleaning expunged the past and brought order to the present. Yet the future was so messy, so murky for my father. A dark parasite was consuming his wife, sullying her flesh. No amount of scrubbing was going to redeem my father or heal my mother.

~

"Look at me," my mother said while staring into a wide mirror over the sink in the upstairs bathroom of our gray house. She was in a white, ankle-length nightgown with slender straps over the shoulders.

It was early morning, and I was still rubbing sleep from my twelve-year-old eyes.

"No man would want to have this." Her arms crossed her chest as her fingers slid along scars on her shoulders. "No man would touch this, touch me."

I looked at her face in the mirror. Her eyes seemed to be retreating. The chemotherapy made her cheeks swell and her once-wide smile shrink.

"Don't you think—" Her words, like her body, were caught somewhere in the mirror. "Don't you think I should feel the touch of another man before I die? But no man wants me, wants this."

I thought of my father, three-thousand miles away with another woman, a new wife with a body that tanned instead of becoming bloated or bruised or struggling to reconcile with itself. I thought about how he had exchanged one faulty body for a ten-year-younger, palatable mass of flesh, one without blemishes, without faded patches of skin or mud-colored lumps. I knew of no man to call and ask to embrace my mother, to hold her affectionately and tell her she was a beautiful woman. I knew of no man who could comfort my mother or make her smile or tell her, *It will be alright. We can make it through this together.* So I turned around and shuffled back to my bedroom, leaving her alone with the mirror. Then I knelt near my bed, buried my head in my clasped hands, and prayed for a tall, strong man to come to my house and hug and hold and protect my mother, to be by her side at the hospital and at the dinner table, sharing a colorful story or a poor joke, possibly bringing a trace of joy to a despairing woman.

My prayers were never answered. The only men to show up at our house and stay more than five minutes were my uncles and my grandfather. There were many womenfolk visiting the home, though. When my mother began her chemotherapy treatments, which slowly broke her body, she decided to join a book group, a macrame group, a Tupperware group, a cosmetic group, filling her remaining days with a potent combination of Catholicism, women's work, women's talk, women's laughter, and scholarship. She maintained her trips to the confessional but also journeyed to the classroom, enrolling in courses at the local community college, where she worked and studied when she felt fit enough.

~

"STEVE, SCHOOL IS THE MOST IMPORTANT THING. Promise me you will go to college right after you graduate. Don't wait like me. I should've gone to college right out of high school. Don't make my mistake," my mother told me one evening.

I did not know if these words were for my benefit or hers, so I simply nodded in agreement. She was working and attending classes as much as her body would allow, yet I sensed she was unsure about how long she could continue both: continue with her sorority-like meetings, and continue with her childrearing single-handedly.

We were sitting at the kitchen table, constructing a Spanish-American War project for my sixth-grade history class. My mother had just helped me make two molasses cakes for the whole class. Before he left, my father had been diligent about keeping up with the latest from Encyclopedia Brittanica, updating the collection on an annual basis. I found those volumes to be indispensable in my upbringing. When I discovered that American soldiers had used molasses in their food because of a tariff on sugar during the Spanish-American War, I asked my mother to help me make molasses cakes, enough for the whole class.

While the two cakes cooled, I hauled my mother's sewing chest, which weighed nearly as much as I did at the time, to the kitchen table and started piecing together a uniform based on a picture from the encyclopedia of a turn-of-the-century American soldier. I had decided to dress one of my G.I. Joes as though he was a typical soldier fighting in the Spanish-American War. My nineteenth-century G.I. would be part of a presentation alongside the molasses cakes he might have eaten, the uniform he wore—a hand-sewn navy blue hat included—and all the gear: a canteen and bayonet made from salt dough, a patch of plaid wool for a miniature bed roll tied to a hand-sewn brown backpack, a whittled stick for a rifle, and G.I. Joe boots painted black.

"Let me teach you how to sew." My mother studied the picture of the soldier in the encyclopedia. "Why don't I do the soldier's jacket, and you sew his pants while copying what I do?"

We worked for about an hour on the uniform in complete silence. It was tedious work. I kept looking at my mother's stitches, yet I was drawn to her face. She wore thick, black-rimmed glasses for reading, which obscured much of the sullenness in her eyes. She would glance at her stitches then to the picture, sewing while reading about war and politics and death.

"More men died from disease than from battle in this war," my mother said. "How awful."

Disease was such a mystery to me at such a young age; I had merely glossed over that fact while reading, thereby conjuring only images of the sweaty marches and intense battles and restless, most likely grateful-to-be-alive souls sleeping under the stars. Upon hearing my mother's statement about disease, I thought of how inglorious and shameful contracting Yellow Fever must have been for those fighting men serving their country during time of war. My heart sank terribly, too.

~

THE MORNING AFTER my father departed from our gray house, I helped my mother set up an electric typewriter at the kitchen table. It was a bulky, pale machine with keys sensitive to the touch. I plugged the machine into a wall socket while my mother sat and fed a piece of blank white paper into the machine.

"I need to put food on the table," she murmured before she began typing her resume.

The machine hummed while my mother rapidly moved her fingers along the keys. I was amazed how swiftly she typed and rapped the metal return bar before a dull ding sounded. Each letter was a thud against paper as metal arms reached out to form sentences my mother had not thought about for sixteen years.

She had some clerical experience, working for an insurance

company after graduating from high school, but once she was married, she left the idea of a career behind. Throughout her sixteen-year marriage, her work encompassed three demanding children, maintaining a modest home, managing her own disappointment toward a wayward, feckless husband, and confronting the horrors of an unexpected, terminal illness.

It took her less than a week to get an interview at Corning Community College.

"It isn't much, but it will keep us fed and the lights on," she said excitedly, beaming with pride after she was offered a job.

~

MY MOTHER CALLED HER FAMILY often after the divorce. She spoke to at least one of her parents or siblings every day. Each phone conversation included a plea to return home, a return to Waterbury. My mother refused to entertain the notion as if it were a shameful proposition, a sign of failure. She would often tell my grandfather, a tremendously persuasive and venerable man, that everything was alright in the hope of assuaging his fears and his doubts, yet he knew his youngest daughter was determined not to return until she had fixed everything that was broken after the day she had left her loving home in Waterbury.

"Dad, we are fine!" Mom would shout. She had to shout because Bump was losing his hearing; therefore, no matter where we were in the house, Chris, Kev, and I were privy to our mother fending off our grandfather's pleas. *I have a job now... The children have friends here... And school... And sports... We are not moving... No, Dad, you don't need to send money... I had Richard's pay garnished... And I am working... If I need anything, I will ask you... Yes, Dad, I'll pray for you, too...*

For years, up until her death, my mother's family tried to

convince her to leave a house so gray. Perhaps such a move, a return home, compromised my mother's determination to overcome cancer, divorce, and money woes on her own terms. She still clung to a Rockwellian vision of an idyllic American family—all freckled-faced and nestled along a cul-de-sac—working together toward the singular purpose of being as autonomous as possible, beholden only to God and country. This dream, which permeated my childhood, melded with our Catholic faith and produced a series of new rituals for my mother. She made sure the mortgage on our humble gray home was paid on time, taxes were paid on time, the brown battleship was maintained and full of gas, the lawnmower was cleaned, oiled and full of gas, and the fridge remained full of food, if only for one day.

~

WE SPENT MANY OF OUR SATURDAY MORNINGS clipping coupons as a family. My sister, brother, and I were allowed to clip coupons for our favorite junk food—Cap'n Crunch and Lucky Charms and Hostess Twinkies and Hostess CupCakes and Jell-O pudding—while my mother handled the coupons for toiletries and frozen vegetables. My mother was highly organized. She kept all the coupons in a plastic index card flip-top box with categories: meat, veggies, snacks, etc. Sometimes I thumbed through the coupon box to see what I could get, and if there was no coupon for something I wanted, I argued with my mother.

"Can't we get Count Chocula cereal, please? And Swanson Salisbury Steak TV dinners?"

"Are there coupons for them?"

"No."

"Well, if you pay for it, then I will buy it," my mother responded each and every time I pleaded. The pleas were part performance and part frugality on my part.

Inevitably, I ran up to my room, crawled under my bed, and pulled out a small metal lock box that contained my most cherished items: a foldable ice skate lace tightener with a tan handle, a slingshot, a brown ceramic chess piece—a bishop—I made in middle school, a wallet-size picture of Cathy Leiser (my first bona fide girlfriend), a wallet-size picture of Terri Mathis (my second bona fide girlfriend, if a courtship lasting less than forty-eight hours counts), a small 8mm reel of my parents' wedding, which I found in a box in our cellar that my mother planned to discard, and a blue cloth pouch filled with my earnings from my paper route (my first bona fide job). I would shake three or four quarters from my blue pouch, slide my tiny treasure chest back under my bed, scurry back down the stairs, and give my mother the coins.

"Okay, come with me and you can pick out what you want at the store."

My mother liked to buy a week's-worth of groceries every Saturday. Cashiers were patient souls, plodding through dozens of coupons then filling paper bags to the rim. Once we got home, I liked to help my mother unpack, even though it was a dangerous chore. She knew I was excited to start snacking on junk food, but this food came with a warning from my mother, who lectured sternly, interjecting apocalyptic visions.

"Stephen, don't go eating all the Twinkies now and ruining your supper, those TV dinners you wanted. This food needs to last us a week. That means there is no going back to the store until next Saturday. If you eat all the Fluffernutter, all the bologna and bread, you'll have nothing to bring to school to eat."

Predictably, my siblings and I devoured all the junk food by Sunday evening, and my mother kept her promise. Aside from the occasional venture to a nearby convenient store for milk, Mom refused to return to the grocery store until Saturday arrived again. Consequently, we ate well as a family after the cupboards were cleared of Hostess treats and sugared cereals and marshmallow Fluff.

Our mother taught us about frugality while Gram taught us a different kind of thrift—how to cook wholesome meals with the most meager of ingredients.

"Chrissy, you can turn a one-dollar steak into a ten-dollar meal," Gram liked to say to my sister when we sat down to eat.

While my mother received treatment on and off for three years at Roswell Park Comprehensive Cancer Center in Buffalo, Gram relied heavily on my sister's curiosity in the kitchen, my determination to keep the lawnmower in a straight line, and Kev's love for our dog, Muffet. That dog followed him everywhere. Even to the football field.

~

THE DAY MY MOTHER RETURNED home from her first encounter with chemotherapy, spring had taken hold of our hamlet and the streets had been swept clean, which signaled Easter was nearly upon us. In our house, Easter felt like a second Christmas; presents were hidden throughout the house and bountiful baskets of candy and cards greeted us first thing in the morning. Every Easter, my mother rose early, cunningly stashing gifts throughout our gray house. Mom also proudly prepared three white rattan baskets for Chris, Kev, and me, filling them with large milk chocolate bunnies and Hallmark cards from our aunts who generously enclosed two dollars in cash or two-dollar McDonald's coupons. Then she cooked an enormous breakfast. Before opening the cards or eating breakfast or going to church, we hunted for our presents, rifling through closets, searching inside the washer and dryer, peering under the sofa and wicker furniture. If we could not find our present, Mom offered clues, chuckling, enjoying her wit and wile as we desperately searched for our Easter surprise. But after she returned from Buffalo, Mom's wits were clouded by cytotoxins. She appeared as gray as our house, a smoky spirit barely burning.

The following morning, I walked downstairs and shuffled into the kitchen to eat breakfast before catching the school bus. Gram was at the sink, staring out of the window. She had her apron on, ready for a day of cooking and cleaning, offering my mother a respite. I stood behind Gram for a moment. She was scrubbing mugs and plates. My presence went unnoticed, so I turned and opened a cupboard casually and grabbed a box of Lucky Charms.

Our mother had instituted an evening routine early on, so we did not have to rush through breakfast before school. We had strict bedtimes and perfunctory obligations before we were able to climb into our crisply tucked beds. The three of us had to take baths, lay out our clothes for school the next day, and say our prayers. Sometimes these evening prayers were hurried, such as a rapid (*Lord's Prayer*), allowing me to hop into bed, turn on my Walkman, and listen to the rock group Styx, either the *Paradise Theater* or *Grand Illusion* cassette while I dreamt of Cathy Leiser or Terri Mathis or both simultaneously. Sometimes my evening prayers were rambling distress signals to God or ardent prayers for my heart to heal from unrequited love.

The evening ritual was easiest on my brother. He did not need to decide what to wear the next day to school because he wore the same outfit each and every day: a blue sweatshirt, faded blue jeans, blue wristbands, a clean pair of tube socks, and clean underwear. Usually, when Gram visited, she would ball-up his only outfit at night after he put on his pajamas. Then she washed his school clothes—which were his play clothes, too—each morning, long before my brother and I woke.

The only challenge in the morning for my brother was the taming of his cowlick. Kev was never a vain child—on the contrary, he was rather opposed to fastidiousness. But he spent many mornings in front of the bathroom mirror sternly combing his cowlick into submission. He simply desired that the hair on his head be obedient. Unfortunately, most mornings were difficult for my brother, who tortured his cowlick as if it were a prisoner of war.

As Gram wistfully looked beyond through the kitchen window, I poured a healthy amount of Lucky Charms into a bowl. When I turned to get the milk from the refrigerator, I heard a retching sound. I took several steps toward the laundry room near the kitchen. Beyond the washer and dryer was a half-bathroom. The door was wide open. My mother was on her knees, vomiting violently into the toilet. My sister, a freshman in high school, was kneeling next to my mother. She was rubbing her back gently, telling my mother she would be *okay*.

Then my mother retched uncontrollably again. She looked and sounded like everything inside of her needed to escape from her body, as if she were turning inside out, imploding like thousands of soapy bubbles in a bath. My sister turned and looked at me. "She'll be okay. Everything will be okay."

I stood blinking and slouching, befuddled by my mother's groans while my sister rubbed her back calmly.

Mornings like this persisted for many weeks. My sister, a volunteer candy striper, became my mother's caregiver while Gram made sure meals were prepared and Kev and I were doing our homework and chores. Sometimes my sister did both: She cared for our mother and made dinner while Gram went to the grocery store. An immense amount of responsibility was heaped on my sister's shoulders. Luckily, like Kev and I, Chris took out much of her angst playing sports. She was rarely seen without a tennis racket in her hand or slung over her shoulder. As we got older, and as our mother slowly declined, a court or a field became a refuge where the three of us wore our bodies out, draining our own vitality so we would be able to feel nothing—not rage, not guilt, not regret—when we returned to the gray house after practices or games.

Sports offered friendship, too, and my sister tended to lean on a wide swath of friends. She knew intimately more than me about how much pain our mother endured from the chemotherapy. She also knew intimately more than me about how much our mother's heart broke after the divorce. Chris knew she could not heal such wounds or console our mother in ways that ameliorated a body or a soul. It was her friends who buoyed her, offering solace from the gray house on Meadow Lane.

As much as my sister understood our mother's illness, the heartbreak was a different dilemma altogether. None of us could have known the depth of our mother's shame regarding the divorce unless we were in the confessional with her. In the eyes of the Catholic Church, marriage was a sacred covenant and breaking such a bond was a sin. Therefore, my mother considered herself to be a sinner, even though it was her husband who had committed adultery on several occasions, not her. She sought redemption from Father Rogers, and she also consulted Father Logue, the priest who had married my parents. Even though Father Rogers and Father Logue absolved my mother of her sin of divorce, the shame she inherited stirred doubts about her entrance into Heaven, a quandary that weighed heavily on her mind during her remaining days.

~

Gram remained for several weeks, helping my mother recoup from her first course of chemo, moving into my brother's and my bedroom while Kev and I turned the Hide-A-Bed sofa into a fort equipped with sleeping bags, flashlights, and canteens full of Hawaiian Punch. We also turned our family room into a war zone. As if we were Audie Murphy and John Wayne, Kev and I leapt over furniture, firing off cap guns, revolvers and bolt-action rifles; it was the Wild West; it was Iwo Jima; it was Normandy; it was Gettysburg. We slammed into chairs as if they were sandbag bunkers and performed dramatic yet heroic death scenes. We made war in our family room as our dog, Muffet, howled mournfully only a few feet away while the cap guns popped and smoked and one of us clutched our imaginary wounds.

Muffet was allowed to sleep with us at night. She helped us devour pans of Jiffy Pop popcorn while we traded goofy stickers found in Wacky Packages until we fell asleep. No matter how loud the ruckus downstairs, our mother remained in her bedroom, only leaving when she was overwhelmed by nausea. For several weeks, she retched violently on her knees while her head bobbed up and down like a yoyo over the toilet bowl. She heaved and heaved. My sister often held her head or rubbed her back. Most of the time nothing came out except for her prayers; *please give me strength.*

When Easter morning arrived, I ran into the kitchen. Gram stood with an apron stretched snuggly across her church clothes, flipping flapjacks on a griddle. A smattering of rouge was on each cheek, ornate earrings hung from her lobes, a white-beaded necklace dangled over the apron. She moved with purpose, unencumbered by high heel shoes.

Three large milk chocolate bunnies were still in their boxes standing near the griddle on the counter.

"I am going to search for my present."

"Dearie."

I stopped and swung around before tearing through the house.

"The Easter Bunny was in a rush this morning, so he dropped your presents off with me, and I'll give them to you after church." She noticed my disappointment. "You can have your chocolate bunny while I get the pancakes ready."

Mom never missed a Mass when she was home, not in the hospital, until this Easter Sunday. She had the habit of laying out our clothes on Saturday nights, feeding us quickly on Sunday mornings, then corralling us into the bathroom where she scrubbed off any visible grime and firmly combed knots from our hair. Miraculously, she always found time to dress, tidy her own hair, prepare a modest offering (two dollars) in an envelope, and hustle us to the car. But not this Easter Sunday.

When we returned from Easter Mass with Gram, Mom moved slowly down the stairs as we burst into the house, excited to hunt for our presents. Mom clutched the railing with one hand while her other hand gripped her ribs tightly. She was wearing a fuzzy blue bathrobe and white slippers. She labored mightily with each step, struggling to remain upright. I thought she was going to slip or trip or collapse.

"Happy Easter." She smiled.

"Chrissy, go get the bag on the bed in my room." Gram was smiling, too.

We sat on the wicker furniture in our small living room near the entryway and stairs. Our father had forbidden Kev and me to sit in the living room for fear our rough nature might destroy the delicate wicker. He was correct. After this unique Easter, when we were granted permission to play in the living room, Kev and I slowly destroyed the furniture, ruining two wicker chairs, a wicker love seat, a wicker coffee table, and a wicker ottoman. Several years of practicing goal-line offense—whereby we lined up the wicker furniture like the defensive line of the Pittsburgh Steelers and rammed through or leapt over the *Steel Curtain*, in this case the *Wicker Curtain*—turned the furniture into rickety pieces of woven twigs. At the time, Kev and I did not grasp the irony of our rough response to an absent father.

From the bag my sister fetched, Gram pulled out a Barry Manilow album for Chris and handed it to her.

"As homely as that man is, he sure sings beautifully," my mother said, smiling at my sister.

Chris leapt from her chair, gave Mom a kiss, and hurried up to her room to listen to her new album. Loving everything Barry Manilow, my sister had forced the entire family to endure his special performances on television, which were colorful if not ostentatious.

Gram pulled out a junior-size basketball and handed it to me.

"Is that what you wanted?" Mom asked me as I ripped away the cardboard packaging.

I nodded and gripped the ball, able to hold it with one of my twelve-year-old hands. "Gram, I think there is another gift for Steve, and a couple of things for Kev."

Gram handed Kev and me each a package of red-white-and-blue sweatbands for our wrists.

"Aw, thanks, Mom," Kev and I said simultaneously.

"I don't want to see any more bruises or cuts on your wrists after you play this *slam ball*."

"We call it *Jam Ball*, Mom." Kev and I laughed.

"Well, whatever you call it, I don't want to hear anymore complaining about your wrists hurting when you *jam* the ball in those low baskets."

"You *slam* the ball into the basket, Mom, like a *slam dunk*, but we call it *Jam Ball*."

"I don't care what you and your friends call it. I just don't want to hear anymore whining about your wrists."

Kev and I laughed again. Our mother broke into a smile as well. Then Gram handed my brother a football. Kev immediately started cradling it in his arms.

Kev and I jumped out of our chairs, gave our mother the quickest of kisses, and ran upstairs to change into our play clothes.

~

Gram left shortly after Easter. She was flying to Germany to see my uncle Harry's family, who I only knew from photos Gram shared. Seeing younger cousins playing with exotic toys or walking along a sidewalk with unusual trees or sitting with Gram in a wingback chair while reading an unfamiliar book, forced me to imagine a world much different than my own, a place Gram traveled to at least once a year since her son, Harry, had been assigned to an United States Air Force base near Frankfurt. Curiously, she never traveled to California to see my father; therefore, without pictures provided by Gram, or my father for that matter, I ended up conjuring an imaginary place where the sun shone perpetually, striking all the people it touched harshly, poisoning their flesh like my mother's. There was no reprieve by night. The sun was as permanent as the air my father continued to inhale while lying in bed next to his second wife, who he married shortly after my mother's first round of chemotherapy.

Oddly, I felt more connected to my relatives in Germany than my father in California. He called once a month, but if my mother answered the phone, her venom oozed defensively, angrily, and my father would wait several more months before calling again. These phone conversations between us were short and awkward.

"When are you coming home?"

"I am not."

"Why?"

"I have a job here, in San Jose."

And this was the extent of our interactions—my father explaining his notion of home simply as a place where one works, not where one's children reside.

There were days my father's absence felt good, especially when it was raining outside and my brother and I lined up the wicker furniture for indoor football practice. It felt good to recklessly crash into objects our father had banned, bouncing off the forgiving furniture. Of course, our mother did not permit us to abuse the wicker furniture. We punished things while Mom was fast asleep, when her beleaguered body became inert and her mind swam hazily from the multitude of pain medications.

~

A few weeks after Gram left for Germany, Kev grabbed his new football and we jetted out of the house without telling our mother where we were going because we did not want to wake her on a sunny Saturday morning. We cut through neighbors' lawns, gathered our friends, and fled our homes to play a football game at *The Churchyard*, a sprawling, level field only a five-minute walk from our home. A small, dark brown Protestant church abutted the field, sitting dormant except for an hour or so on Sunday mornings. Compared to my Sunday morning experiences at Immaculate Heart of Mary, few parishioners attended service at the tiny, brown church.

Epic games were played at *The Churchyard*, where boys—and a few brawny girls—became brutes, smashing and tackling one another as if our bodies were malleable clay, folding and unfurling from fierce collisions. Often older neighbors, high schoolers, caught glimpses from their windows of the rabble tossing a football as it paraded toward *The Churchyard*. They joined in the procession. Once at the field, a couple of teenagers anointed themselves captains, picking my brother first each time. He happened to be the most adroit kid in the neighborhood, slippery like a greased piglet who ran like a gazelle. No one could ever get a firm grip on him, and if someone did, somehow my brother danced out of the tattered, blue, sleeveless sweatshirt he always wore. One of us was usually left standing with Kev's sweatshirt in his hands while he galloped for a touchdown. Trying to tackle my brother was like lassoing a honey badger—he was utterly unstoppable with a football in his hands. It took a swarming gang to bring him down.

When we were in the midst of starting the game on a sunny Saturday morning, Muffet appeared. Kev was running with the football, twirling around floundering tacklers when Muffet entered the fray and began barking and nipping at our friends' ankles. She was about the size of a honey badger, yet I had never seen her act combative before. Kev stopped, and my friend Dion tackled him. They both fell to the ground. Muffet growled and snapped at Dion.

"Get this crazy damn dog away from me!"

I grabbed Muffet and pulled her away from Dion. When I let go, she assailed Dion again, so I grabbed her by the collar and started to drag her home. She resisted. It was like pulling a broken-wheeled wagon. I yanked her along, clutching her by the scruff of her neck; my body was hunched over and pissy from sweat. Once we got to the house, I opened the front door, slung her inside, swung the door shut, and ran quickly back to the game, wondering why Muffet was acting so strangely. She was such a good-natured dog, allowed to roam the neighborhood without a leash. Neighbors did not complain if she sauntered into their yard slowly and gracelessly with her short legs and long ears dragging–no one begrudged her a leisurely visit.

A short time after I returned to *The Churchyard*, Muffet appeared again, galloping into the middle of our game, snarling at Kev's friend McFall this time, who was chasing after Kev as he heaved the football as far as he could. It landed with a thud.

"Muffet, Goddammit, go!" Kev yelled.

Muffet kept after McFall, who was running in circles like a Keystone Cop, screaming dramatically as if a real honey badger was at his heels. Kev sprinted to Muffet, grabbed her by the collar, and hauled her home. Kev's team did not want to play without him, so they called for a halftime break. Some of us ran over to the convenient store near the church. We bought bottles of Orange Crush and Big Red cherry pop, slugging the sweet sodas down while waiting for Kev.

No sooner had we started the second half of the football game when Muffet showed up for the third time, causing as much chaos as the first two fracases. I snatched her collar but not before she took a swipe at my friend Jay's trousers.

"I'll beat that damn dog with the football if I have to!" Jay shouted while smiling.

I hauled Muffet home. This time I picked her up and carried her with both arms like a pile of laundry. She wiggled and flailed as I jogged home. Not wanting to miss anymore of the game, I held onto her tightly while she bounced in my tired arms.

"Mom, are you awake?" I yelled, standing at the foot of the stairs, breathing heavily, waiting for a response. I heard her bedroom door open. My mother appeared at the top of the stairs. She was wearing a nightgown.

"Yes, what is it?"

"Mom, can you keep Muffet inside? We're trying to play a football game at *The Churchyard*, and she keeps interfering."

Muffet stood beside me, innocently looking up at me. I was *ratting* her out.

"She's been sitting at that door, howling all morning. I can't get any sleep. You take her with you or you stay here with her. I am not going to listen to her howl anymore." My mother abruptly turned. Then her bedroom door slammed shut.

It was the end of another epic game at *The Churchyard*.

~

My mother was slowly regaining strength, slowly recovering an appetite after the first course of chemotherapy. Although her body was bloated and pale, she began to smile more and attend church regularly, rallying us on Sunday mornings once again. Yet under her eyes, a darkness had gathered; deep blotches the color of coal had materialized, which she covered with thick dollops of Avon concealer before going out in public. My mother did her best to mask any melancholy under her eyes for the remainder of her life.

Mom became an Avon Lady after her stamina fully returned. She sold beauty products to neighbors, coworkers, and friends, making a little extra cash and stockpiling a surplus of makeup.

"I just sold Ms. Russo sixteen-dollars-worth of makeup. That's four dollars for us," Mom said to me one day before even greeting me with a *hello, how was practice?*

I was on my bike, a Huffy with a banana seat the color of a bumblebee, peddling madly to get home after baseball practice because I was famished. I had to slam on the brakes, skidding the bike to a stop at the end of our driveway so I did not crash into my mother, who was carrying a large, mauve Avon sample case. She was smiling.

"Did you know she is a single mother too?"

I did. Ms. Russo's son, Victor, was a year younger than me and had once said, *My father's not around.* Being a good Catholic at the time, I did not want to pry into his personal life, so I'd just shrugged and left it at that.

"You should be nicer to Victor. I don't wanna hear about you being mean to him." My mother's face went from delight to disappointment.

"Okay." I hopped off my bike and began pushing it up the driveway. I was not entirely certain what my mother's missive meant. Victor liked being inside, liked being alone. My brother and I were able to lure Victor out to play occasionally, but Victor did not like football or basketball or baseball. He did like to wear black shirts and black pants, though, even during the most sultry of summer days.

He was the first friend we made when we moved to Corning. His house was only two doors down. My brother and I enjoyed his company and encouraged him to come out and play. Of course it was rough play with rough language and rough tempers—a game of *kill the carrier* usually involved injury (just bruises or cuts or sprains), and the game *the thing*, which I had concocted based on a movie, involved chasing a monster with toy guns, which Victor did not have permission to play with, so, inevitably, he was picked to be the monster. As boys, our bodies were not holy temples nor were they evil. On the contrary, they were wonderment: How pliable, dexterous, willful and durable could our bodies become? Victor did not like being the monster—no one did—so I imagined he must have told his mother we liked to chase him with guns.

~

When my mother was not working for the college or hocking Avon products, she was hosting Tupperware parties in our home to make ends meet. She earned a small commission from each item of Tupperware sold, peddling plastic to our neighbors and friends. She also received free gifts: kitchen utensils, tumblers, lunch boxes, things that were unbreakable in the hands of my brother or me. For a young boy, it was a bizarre scene to witness a dozen or so grown women with well-cultivated hairdos huddled around plastic bowls and plastic pitchers and plastic jelly molds, exchanging recipes and pleasantries. These wonders drank coffee and snacked on tiny tuna sandwiches with pimento olives secured by toothpicks while chatting gregariously at the same time. Muffet milled about, searching for crumbs on the floor. She was unfazed by the clamorous din in our family room.

My mother was in her element, a merry and doting hostess who enjoyed a good guffaw. She was most comfortable in a crowd without having to be the center of attention, and what she lacked in wit, she made up for in sincerity. She listened earnestly to stories of children, of husbands, of work, never revealing her own travails. She kept her heartbreak and her disease stifled, like inhaling a pitiful tear or choking down a cough or swallowing a harmless hiccup—these unpleas-antries were there, swelling within her, while she charmed these women.

Mom was immensely proud of our humble, gray home, and she intended on keeping it. Her three jobs helped supplement a court order directing my father's employer in California to send a check to our home every payday, but it was not enough according to my mother. "Your father makes good money, but he has to support two families now. Things have changed."

I had not met my father's new wife or her daughter from a previous marriage. I learned of their matrimony from my mother after dinner one night when she called a family meeting.

"I need you all to sit down."

Our mother was pensive, so was my brother. He stood in

front of Mom with his arms dangling at his sides and one knee slightly bent.

"Please sit down, Kevin."

Kev was motionless. He was probably thinking the same as me: chemotherapy had not cured our mother.

"Okay." Our mother smirked. "Your father has remarried." She looked at her hands and folded her fingers together in her lap.

We were stunned into silence, a deadening stillness. Until...

"Well, fuck that!" Kev stormed out of the house.

I never discovered where my brother went on these fretful occasions. He may have been weeping in the garage or attic, or peddling his bike furiously around the neighborhood, or chucking a ball against the cement wall at the park. But he always returned at sundown, bereft of words and tears. I never saw my brother cry, not once, not even after our mother died. But the pain was there, barely underneath the skin of a boy who always seemed to be in motion, condemning inertia as if it were a distant place or a terminal disease.

"Geez, Mom, you think we didn't know he was going to do this? He kept saying how unhappy he was in this house when you two dragged us to those family therapy sessions," Chris said placidly. Her cheeks were fully flushed. "Why would anyone want to live in this house?" Chris rose from the worn, brown recliner. "I am going upstairs. I've got a lot of homework to do. It's one thing after another around here."

I sat next to my mother, slouching and blinking and recalling those family therapy sessions when I'd keep my head down, trying to turn invisible, slowly melting into the hard plastic chair I slumped meekly in. We had been in a large room but much of the space had been engulfed by heated arguments between my parents. After every question posed to me by the therapist, I had shrugged and focused on my scrawny legs dangling from an uncomfortable seat.

Sanctuary for my sister was her room, her records, her schoolwork, a tennis court. Sanctuary for my brother and me was *The Churchyard*, the basketball court, the baseball diamond. Sanctuary for my father was anywhere but home. Sanctuary for my mother was church and a concept of home she clung to desperately. Therapy only exacerbated what my sister surmised at a young age: There is sanctity in solitude.

"Steve, do you have any questions for me?"

Sitting next to my mother on the plaid couch, I craned my head and looked at her. She was biting her lower lip. Her hands were still folded in her lap. Her eyes were two blue question marks. What I would have given at that moment to offer my hand, to gently fold my fingers into hers, to place my head on her shoulder and softly say, *It will be alright, everything will be alright, another man will fall for you, will marry you, will cherish you.* Instead, I shrugged and blinked.

"Do you ever think Dad will come to see one of my baseball games?" I asked.

"I don't know." My mother caressed my hair, and her eyes became soft and watery. "Maybe."

~

MY MOTHER MUST HAVE MENTIONED something to my father because a package arrived a few days before my first Little League Baseball game. It was an early—four months early—birthday present: a Wilson first baseman's glove. My mother brimmed when I opened the package, put her hand on my shoulder, and offered a gentle kiss on my towhead. I immediately slid the glove on my right hand and pounded the pocket where the palm rests. It was slightly big for my twelve-year-old hand, but I had a batting glove that would make it fit more snuggly. The leather smelled like warm bread, and the fingers felt smooth, like a hardbound book cover.

"Can I go get glove oil?"

My father had taught me how to break in a baseball mitt and create the perfect pocket, which involved a baseball, rope, and meticulous oiling of the glove.

"Do you have the money to pay for it?"

"Yes."

I ran to my room, pulled my metal lock box from under my bed, and poured quarters into the fingers of my new baseball glove. Then I jumped on my Huffy with the bumblebee-colored banana seat, hung the glove on the handlebars, and sped a mile to our local department store, Nichols, the same store where my baseball coach, Mr. Woods, worked behind a counter in the hunting and fishing section, doling out fishing lures to my friends and me in the summer. He was a wiry fellow with a thick, brown mustache and slits for eyes; a soft-talking and soft-walking man who had a son, Michael, on the team.

"Coach, look at my new mitt." I held it above the counter where Mr. Woods stood, drumming his fingers on a glass case filled with various serrated knives and boxes of bullets. "What do you think?"

"I like it." He nodded and smiled.

"My dad just sent it to me. Look, see, it has the flat pocket for scooping the ball. I don't think a ball will get by me, it's so big. I can't wait to play. I can't wait for Saturday," I said rapidly as if my entire body suddenly became feverish. "I am gonna get some glove oil, Coach, and break it in, so I'll see you Saturday."

That night I strategically placed a baseball—some people preferred the web, some preferred the pocket, but I opted for the web crotch, an area in between—in the heavily-oiled glove and wrapped it tightly with a yard of my mother's cord for macrame. I slept with the glove beside me.

After school the next day, my brother impersonated Vida "True" Blue and Ron "Louisiana Lightning" Guidry in our backyard. He threw the baseball as hard as he could into my waiting glove while I squatted like a catcher, providing a big target and straining to scoop the ball if it hit the ground.

After dinner, I folded the glove and squatted on it like a hen while watching TV until bedtime. It was hard to fall asleep the night before my first game with my new mitt wrapped in macrame cord beside me as I lay in bed. I prayed for hours, imploring God to not make it rain. I dreamt of the field, its diamond shape, its pale dirt and groomed grass. My father, like mist, was stirring behind the dugout, smoking a cigarette, chatting with Coach Woods. I began to cry.

When Saturday morning arrived, my glove felt light and soft, well-broken in. I put on my bright orange baseball uniform before breakfast and waited for my mother and sister. They volunteered to work in the concession stand on Saturday mornings during the Little League season. My sister dutifully helped my mother open the stand before the first game. They worked the entire day, selling hotdogs, candy, and soda. Other mothers and daughters volunteered, too. It was a time to socialize as much as it was about feeding families ballpark treats.

Mom snuck away to see a few innings of our game. Kev and I were on the same team sponsored by the local credit union. He was the only ten-year-old player in the major division and the only left-handed shortstop I had ever seen play the position. He liked to pitch as well, and if we were winning by a large margin, Coach had him play centerfield because Kev liked covering left and right field if necessary. My mother, wearing her enormous sunglasses, sat in the stands and mingled, never shouting a word of encouragement or discouragement while we played. Like her days as a high school cheerleader, Mom cared more about being among friends and neighbors than the outcome of the game. She liked to quote the humorist Erma Bombeck—*Life is a bowl of cherries with many pits*—if my team lost a game or if I was disappointed with my performance on the field of play. Bombeck's words never ameliorated my frustrations, but they made Mom giggle.

After the game, my mother fed Kev and me hotdogs for lunch. Then we were scorekeepers or public address announcers for other games while Mom and Chris served our neighbors, most of whom knew that my father was forced to step down as the President of Corning Painted Post Little League because he had been caught embezzling money made from sponsorships and walkathon fundraisers and the concession stand. He had been caught just before he fled to California.

~

ANOTHER PACKAGE ARRIVED FROM CALIFORNIA several months later, just before I left for Camp Gorton, a Boy Scout summer camp on Lake Waneta about thirty miles north of Corning. It was a large box, almost as tall as me, yet light enough for my mother, whose body was less swollen and fatigued, to carry to the family room where I slumbered on the sofa, twisting a Rubik's Cube.

"Your father sent an early Christmas present to you," my mother said as she gently laid the box on its back.

I jumped from the sofa, tore into the box, and pulled out a rust-colored Coleman Peak backpack with a flexible black plastic frame, a novel feature that captured my imagination: a backpack the color of Mars' mountains; a backpack designed by NASA; a backpack worthy of display at the National Air and Space Museum. I could not wait to show the guys in the scout troop my brand new, futuristic backpack. I immediately unzipped all the compartments.

"I can put my Sterno stove here, my bedroll there, my pocketknife here, my collapsible cups there, my cooking gear here," I excitedly told my mother. I began to imagine myself as a soldier more equipped than those serving in the Revolutionary or Spanish-American War. I slung the pack on my back. It had a large, padded belt for my waist that hung below my crotch; adjustments needed to be made. "I should call Dad."

"He's at work, honey. Remember there is a time difference. It's only noon in California. You'll have to wait until just before bedtime to call him."

While waiting to call my father, I made several adjustments so the backpack rested comfortable on my slender frame. Then I filled each compartment with camping gear, strapping the bedroll on the top and my sleeping bag on the bottom of the frame; then I tied a full aluminum canteen wrapped in wool to the side of the pack. It was so heavy—at least half my body weight—I had to set the backpack on my bed, rest it against a wall, sit on the bed, and slide my arms through the straps. Then I had to lean forward, crouch like a weightlifter about to snatch a barbell from the ground, and launch myself upward.

I paraded around the house while Mom and Chris made dinner. My shoulders ached from the burden as the weight of the march from the family room to the dining room made my wiry legs wobble. I tried hopping in my hiking boots as if I were crossing a stream, balancing on a rock, vaulting my load and body to the other side. Beads of sweat gathered on my arms and legs. I was a poorly constructed beanpole ready to topple; moreover, I was distressed by the thought of hiking a long distance with all this weight. I began to wonder if Audie Murphy ever complained about the things he carried. I called my father.

"Are you ready for camp?"

"I am."

"Are you ready for your mini-Philmont?"

"Yes, of course." I only thought of the burden on my back, the strain on my shoulders, the ascent and descent of fifty miles of mountainous terrain surrounding Lake Waneta, where a small cohort of Boy Scouts planned to earn numerous merit badges during a five-day excursion of sleeping under the stars or in a self-made lean-to. I had been romanticizing about this adventure for months until the weight of the backpack became close to unbearable. I began to doubt my strength, my endurance.

"Good luck on your hike."

"Thanks."

"Give me a call when you finish the Philmont."

I called my mother, not my father, after the week-long hike that ended up being a seventy-five-mile trek instead of fifty. I told her how our guide, a twenty-something former Eagle Scout named Brad who reeked of marijuana each morning, a detail I left out of the discussion with my mother, led us astray one arduous day. I told her how amazing the hike was, the beauty of the forest and the mountains, how we got lost, how those extra miles on the second day made the rest feel effortless, how comfortable, like a hat or jacket, the backpack eventually became. I was so eager to fill my summer with more adventures that I asked my mother if I could stay another week. She said, *Yes.*

I am not sure how my mother swung the one hundred dollars for the extra week of Boy Scout camp, but it was a most precious gift, a week with one of my best friends, Jay. We stayed in a canvas tent on a wooden platform atop a steep hill, assigned to another troop, perfect strangers who cared little of our whereabouts, so we freely pursued our own interests: swimming, canoeing, capture the flag, wood-carving workshops, greased watermelon relays. We had the glorious freedom to roam among the various fields of play. It was a place of perpetual bliss, a young boy's paradise, Heaven on Earth.

The euphoria after completing a mini-Philmont and a busy yet fun-filled week with Jay took weeks to wear off. I called my father and told him about the hike, about Brad without mentioning marijuana, that Mom had allowed me to stay another week at camp, and that soccer was starting up.

"When will I see you?"

"I have work, Steve, I told you."

~

Since we first grew enough hair on our scalp, our father diligently and painstakingly cut our hair, Kev's and mine. His ability to navigate Kev's cowlick was so impressive we thought our father could never err because he conquered the hairy slope on the side of Kev's forehead with scissors, a comb, and electric clippers. We were mystified, and began worshipping our father, mimicking how he walked or laughed or swam or threw a baseball. Our reverence was steadfast, even after he left the gray house so violently to start another life with a different family.

With our father gone, our mother took over the duties of cutting our hair, but it was obvious she lacked confidence with this new responsibility. In my mind, my mother was never timid or shy. On the contrary, she engaged the world with a hearty smile, immune to embarrassment. But not on this day. On this day she may have been afraid of the unknown, wondering how she could possibly match the reverence her sons had for the man she married. She may have wondered if the boys she bore would be eager to find fault. She may have considered the profundity of how sons transform into men without a father.

She sat me down at the kitchen table, wrapped a worn blue towel around my neck, and kept combing and combing and combing my full head of blond hair. I could hear the television in the family room. It seemed as if three or four music videos had played before my mother picked up the scissors and began to trim and trim and trim blond locks ever so slightly, as if she did not want to disrupt or damage any hair on my head.

"Okay, it looks good to me," my mother said, resting her hands on my shoulders.

She unfastened two clothesline pins and pulled the towel off me. I ran to the bathroom near the kitchen. I looked searchingly into the mirror. I squinted my eyes. I did not see anything uniquely different about my head of hair. It was the exact same as before my mother had picked up the scissors. I did a quick about face then ran to the kitchen. "Can I go outside and play now?"

"Sure. Tell your brother it's his turn now, and be back before dinner." My mother was shaking the towel. I could not see any hair falling off the towel and into the chair.

When I returned home before dinner, Kev was sitting at the kitchen table, wearing the same blue towel wrapped around his shoulders. My mother had a full glass of water in her hand. She was dipping and stirring the comb in the glass as if she were mixing a cocktail, something she rarely consumed. Eventually, she started on my brother's cowlick, combing and combing, dipping and dipping, stirring and stirring, all in hope of pacifying the rogue hairs on my brother's head. Unlike my father, my mother did not have a way of approaching Kev's cowlick.

"Honey, I don't know what to do with this." She grabbed his chin, gently moving it side to side, examining the cowlick from various points of view. She relented.

"I need to make dinner." My mother sighed. "You two can go play for a little while outside."

Weeks later, our mother drove us to a barbershop, a place we had never been. I am sure it was a grueling decision to pay someone else to cut our hair, an expense she did not expect. Luckily, she realized that it was worth the financial sacrifice. Our mother found someone who was an expert in taming cowlicks. Plus, she quickly discovered the barber was a reliable man with sons of his own. His name was Rocky Locey.

Rocky had a small shop in downtown Corning with the motto: "It's not how long you wear it; it's how you wear it long." When we first walked into the barbershop, there was a small, dim-lit waiting area with a table filled with magazines between large cushiony chairs. We sat and I began to rummage through the magazines. My mother sat next to me, leafing through sports, politics, fishing, and hunting magazines.

Rocky casually waved me over to his chair. I climbed a couple of steps to get into the chair at the back of the shop. I had never sat in a barber's chair. My legs dangled as he calmly wrapped a paper choker around my neck then shook a large bib and placed it around my torso, fastening it with a button snap instead of two long clothesline pins securing a worn blue towel.

I immediately noticed Rocky had a tattoo on his arm. He was a tan man, so it was difficult for me to discern the faded image or if there were any words at all. I eventually discovered he had been in the army before moving to Corning. He was affable and much quicker at cutting hair than my father.

"What do you like to do?" Rocky asked.

"I like to play sports."

"What sports do you like?"

"I like football. The Cleveland Browns are my favorite team, the *Cardiac Kids*, Brian Sipe, Ozzie Newsome, and I love baseball, the Pittsburgh Pirates, *We Are Family*, Dave Parker is my favorite player, people call him *The Cobra* because he hits the ball so hard like the way a cobra strikes its prey. My mom let me stay up and watch the whole World Series between the Orioles and Pirates, all seven games. I love to play right field, but my coach makes me play first base like Willie Stargell, but I think I can run faster than him, sometimes I run to the outfield and try to catch the ball and throw it home like Dave Parker does. I almost got a guy out one time."

He didn't say much, just chuckled.

I chuckled, too.

Eventually, after an intuitive vetting process, which relied heavily on many motherly observations over months-worth of haircuts, Mom relinquished full custody to Rocky for one-half hour so she could run errands in downtown Corning while her sons enjoyed the *man's sphere* of a quintessential barbershop. It was impressive how our mother easily accepted Rocky and trusted no harm would come to her sons while away. Plus, she knew Kev and I needed to fill the space vacated by our father, who would foolishly, after our mother's passing, justify his flight to California: "Your mother's cancer was in remission when I left." This assertion sounded like the disease was the only reason for him to stay or that Mom needed to be damaged more than she already was or that she needed to be in pain, needed to be suffering in order for him to stay with us. Our father's justification for leaving plainly confused me.

Much of our time at the barbershop was spent talking about sports. Rocky had five children, two daughters and three sons. One son was a standout quarterback at Bucknell University, and Rocky's youngest son, Lance, was between my grade and Kev's. I ended up playing football with Lance in high school. For me, the barbershop was a man's space where we had ample opportunity to reflect on awe-inspiring athletic feats, such as the Miracle on Ice in 1980, and how a freshman running back named Herschel Walker from the University of Georgia helped win a national championship in that same year. Then a freshman at the University of North Carolina named Michael Jordan hit the winning shot during the college basketball championship in 1981. In 1982, Magic Johnson, a point guard, played center for an injured Kareem Abdul-Jabbar, and led the Los Angeles Lakers to the NBA Championship. Then Doctor J (Julius Erving), my brother's favorite basketball player, went to work and won a well-earned NBA title in 1983, defeating Magic Johnson and the Los Angeles Lakers. How I relished talking, more like babbling, about sports with Rocky, who was patient, listening attentively, kindly nodding, interjecting a lighthearted reflection or two.

After years without seeing my father, I began dreaming about adopting a *new father*, someone more talkative who liked watching sports, someone who would take me camping or fishing. I desperately wanted my *new father* nearby, the one who was full of praise and advice. This *new father* had to help me with my curveball and make sure I did not slouch. This *new father* had to tell my mother, *Everything will be alright.*

~

MY MOTHER HAD TO STOP WORKING when I was in eighth grade and return to Roswell Park Comprehensive Cancer Center in Buffalo for another regimen of chemotherapy. Once again, Gram returned to take care of us. Once again, she showed us pictures of our cousins in Germany where she had spent her summer. They appeared happy—their cheeks flushed like grapefruit.

"You know, Uncle Harry has two families. He was married before he met Donna, before joining the Air Force." Gram retrieved more photos from a shoebox in her lap. She sat on the couch, cradling the images of her summer, sharing stories of food and festivals as well as museums and movie houses. We passed around polaroids of foreign cityscapes and cherubic faces. I was mesmerized by the scenes of playgrounds in Frankfurt; colors seemed brighter, not the gray steel of my childhood. These images, kept in a shoebox, were Gram's gifts to us.

"Uncle Harry's first family lives near me," Gram said.

We knew this, but Gram had never talked about this arrangement before as *Uncle Harry's first family*, which was previously conveyed as *Uncle Harry's older children*, Greggy, Peggy, and Kelly—three cousins rarely mentioned, never seen. Their fate would have been *oblivion* if it were not for Gram, who conjured them from the ether of a dreamworld. Gram fished out more photos from the shoebox and showed us pictures of Kelly posing in front of her house, Greg standing next to his muscle car, and Peggy in a high school graduation gown. Aside from the home, the car, or the gown, they were alone in a forested backdrop.

I began to wonder if this was how Gram might have shared stories of Chris, Kev, and me to others as she passed around photos, Here is Uncle Richard's first family—this is Stevie in his baseball uniform, who likes to carry his first baseman's mitt Dickie bought him all over town in the summer; this is Kevie in his first communion suit, which he didn't like so he is frowning; here is Chrissy in her candy striper uniform—she wants to be a nurse.

I began to feel immensely empty inside, as if I were a solitary subject of a two-dimensional photo without a brother or a sister who were, in reality, sitting only a few feet away from me, peering at Gram's photos. I felt as if I were without a mother, who, in reality, was alone in a hospital many miles away, confined to a bed from potent elixirs meant to destroy the parasites in her body. My father's first family, in reality, was fading away without him, dispersing into a series of separate snapshots, lonely souls captured on film while he was with his second family in a land of unrelenting sun where he parented a small child not made from his own bodily seed.

This loneliness inside me slowly became an erratic companion of mine over time, creating so much ambivalence I did not know whether to mourn the loss of a living father or mourn the loss of a dying mother. At the loneliest of times, I tearfully prayed to God to return my father, even if it meant more crashing casserole dishes. My desperation forced me to make a pact with God: *I will stop it. I will not leave my mother alone in the kitchen with my father. I will protect her, just please, please bring my father home.* These prayers were cris de coeur, a boy's mournful hymn.

At the least lonely of times, I raged at God, demanding that he heal my mother's damaged body. She did not deserve the devilish disease, only *His* compassion. While I prayed, a strength swelled within my own body, as if I were engaged in a battle with a fierce enemy. My prayers became war cries, stern commands for God to act with valor and save my mother's body. At these times, I knelt at my bedside and rocked back and forth with a plastic rosary in my sweaty hands. My incantations were swift, stubborn, ardent pleas: *Save my mother, rid her of disease, take me instead, give me cancer, strike me now.*

There were many nights as a child I crawled into bed feeling hollow, a shadowy figure in a second family, vaguely corporeal, a body fabricated from the gray mist that appears once orange coals are extinguished. Then there were times when my body was flushed, a fabrication of flames, a steely and intense resolve. There was a twoness residing in me, made bearable by sports, Gram's apple pie, and amorous awakenings. Not church. Not prayer. And certainly not psychotherapy.

~

EXCEPT FOR A COUPLE OF SNAFUS in science class that I blamed on Karen Lynch's beauty, I was doing well academically in eighth grade–recommended for ninth grade honors classes in all but science. My mother was not happy with my C in science, but it was too difficult for me to explain how the teacher kept picking Karen Lynch–Venus in the flesh, a tall, buxom blonde with long, immaculate locks–to be my lab partner, which was a thrilling yet destructive occurrence each and every time. Karen liked to toy with her hair and flirt so much I could not concentrate on the simplest of tasks. Even while dissecting a frog, her scent and smile penetrated the formaldehyde-laced innards we poked and prodded together, our hands touching, our bodies glancing, my mind concerned only with her physiology, not the frog's.

Even with my good fortune in the classroom (including my lab partner, Karen) and on a soccer field, basketball court, and baseball diamond, I started drinking alcohol in eighth grade. It started innocently enough–a few sips from half-empty liquor bottles at a friend's house. We were experimenting. Over time, we became daring, bringing bottles of whatever we could get our hands on–vodka, rum, schnapps–to school, turning our bodies numb.

When my mother discovered the twoness inside me– a pensive student-athlete who savored the numbing effects of booze–she demanded I see a headshrinker.

"No sports, no scouts, no school dances ever again unless you meet with the school's psychologist until he says you are cured of this foolish behavior. You will do as I say or you will be grounded for life," my mother said sharply.

This nonnegotiable arrangement served only to further fuel my anger, and I took it out on the unfortunate psychologist, expressing disdain for him from the very first time we met.

"Your mother has shared everything with me. Everything." His eyes grew wide, searching for acknowledgement from me. "Let's start with her. What are your thoughts about her illness, her cancer?"

"I don't know." I shrugged, slouching in a too-big chair with thick armrests. We were in a low-lit, musty office space at Corning Free Academy Middle School.

"Are you worried she is going to die?"

"Yes."

"How does that make you feel?"

"I don't know."

"You know, she really cares about you. She's worried this incident with your buddies and the vodka in the boys' bathroom is because of her illness. What do you think?"

"I don't know."

"Is this the only time you have had a drink of alcohol?"

"No."

"How often do you drink?" His tone was matter of fact, not accusatory like the principal's or like the priest's.

"I don't know." I shrugged and shook my head.

"Do you like to drink?"

"I don't know."

"Okay, well, let's change the subject. Let's talk about your father. How do you feel about your father living in California?"

"I don't know."

"How often do you talk to him?"

"Once a month, maybe."

"Your mother said that after the divorce you got into a lot of fights. Is this true?"

"I don't know, maybe."

"Look, Steve, we are going to be meeting once a week for a while. I understand you don't feel like talking about it, but you have a lot going on—a father who abandoned you and a mother with a serious illness—"

"You don't know shit!" I jumped from the chair. "My father did not abandon me! He calls! He sends me stuff! I just got a brand-new, ten-speed bike in a box from California! It's maroon!

It's awesome!" I walked out and slammed the door.

My mother grounded me for a week. "If you ever act like that again with Mr. Daniels you will be grounded for a lot longer. You will meet with him every week until I say otherwise. You will stay with him for an entire hour, and you will be respectful or you will not watch any of that wrestling stuff on TV Saturday mornings—no television at all, no using the phone, no riding that brand new bike of yours. You'll be upstairs, reading your books until your heart's content."

I pitied the psychologist for having to deal with my hostility, my ignorance, my immaturity, but I sensed he pitied me more, which made me angrier. My teenage body was in disarray, fraught with temptation. And anger.

~

ON A SUNNY SPRING DAY during my eighth-grade year, I sat next to Cathy Balconi on the bus ride home. She was wearing her Catholic school uniform, which required a rather short plaid skirt and a tight white top. There were not enough knee-high socks in all of Corning to cover Cathy's legs, which were golden with a flawless sheen. She rode the public-school bus since Corning's only Catholic school, All Saints Academy, was right around the corner from Corning Free Academy, a two-block walk to her seventh-grade class. She told me that her parents sent her to Catholic school because they did not want boys like me chasing her around all day, distracting her from her studies, and that the nuns rapped the knuckles of boys with wayward eyes. I had merely managed a modest smirk because my cheeks hurt from the pain of embarrassment. She had caught me looking at her legs.

"What are you doing after school?" Cathy asked.

"I have a baseball game," I said, looking down, fearing I

might impulsively leer at her legs.

"I would like to see you play."

"Really?" I snapped my head sideways quickly and looked into her eyes, which were as enticing as her legs: two polished jade stones.

"Yes, really." She smiled. Her brown hair was thick and wavy, whirling above her shoulders.

"Okay," I stammered. "How about I pick you up at four o'clock?"

"Sounds like a date." When she smiled, her dimples turned into two deep caverns I wanted to fall, perhaps stumble, into.

Kev and I were the only ones home after school. Mom was at work and my sister was at tennis practice. I quickly did my homework, then I changed into my uniform, fastidiously tucking in my jersey, cinching my belt, and arranging my cap. When I examined myself in the bathroom mirror, I noticed how my front teeth were two ivory piano keys draped over my bottom lip. Even though I had been wearing a specially designed retainer to align my jaw for three years, my face was still askew. The retainer, my mother said, *Costs a month's-worth of groceries, so you better wear it and not lose it or else you'll be buck-toothed for life and on a bread and water diet for a month.*

I felt like I spent as much time at the dentist's office as I squandered in the psychologist's office. These visits served as reminders that I was a trifle odd—nothing dreadful, but something flawed like a torn seat cushion, functional and comfortable but not necessarily pleasing to the eye.

I stood with my elbows pinned to my sides and my shoulders slumped in front of the bathroom mirror, scrutinizing my gangly, fourteen-year-old body dressed in a maroon baseball uniform. My homely overbite coupled with my pathetic slouching made me look and feel goofy. I asked the mirror, *What girl would ever want this?*

I went to the garage, slung my baseball glove and first base-man's mitt over the handlebars of the bike my father shipped from California—my first ever ten-speed—which was similar to my uniform, a delicious boysenberry color. I hopped on and sped to Cathy Balconi's house only a few cul-de-sacs away, pumping the pedals furiously.

Cathy opened the door before I had a chance to press the doorbell. She wore a white V-neck T-shirt with exceedingly tight white shorts and leather sandals. Without effort, Cathy jumped up onto the bike seat. She sat sidesaddle and held onto my narrow hips as if they were reins for a mule. I stood on the pedals, working hard to maintain our balance as we accelerated. It was only a five-minute bike ride to the baseball field, but it felt much longer, like an extra-inning baseball game. It was an arduous undertaking, having to haul two bodies, shedding my shyness for the sake of breath-shortened conversation and straining from the heat of Cathy's body; her fingers, like conductors, transmitted a sultriness as they grasped me. Pangs grew in my groin, and my protective baseball cup became confining.

During trying times, my youthful body often became mechanical—legs like pistons, and my heart, a combustible motor—as if I were only made of metal and gears, as if my identity were the sum of my vital functions: student, baseball player, son. Perfunctorily, I completed school assignments. Heedlessly, I ran amok on the fields of play. Dutifully, as the eldest son, I honored the family by never revealing its sorrows. Yes, friendship and courtship were important staples, nourishing my body with necessary fuel, yet I never once disclosed my mother's illness or my father's flight to friends or those I pursued romantically. Even when I entered the confessional at church, my body became inert, blinking and silent. It was as if my mother's scarred body and my father's invisible body meant my boyish body was something in-between, something to be punished, preferably on the fields of play, and something to be concealed, preferably by uniforms: sports, scouts, frocks.

Cathy's proximity exposed an awkwardness within me. I wanted to pray right then and there as I labored to keep the bike balanced and our bodies upright, but I worried that God would be angry with me if I requested an embrace or kiss from Cathy. If these were the temptations of a frightful devil, I wanted no part of a wrathful God, so I opted to pray for the strength to carry us both to and from the field. God must have detected my inner thoughts and feelings—a nonsensical notion I passionately believed throughout my youth—for there was sin on the baseball field that day. And I was punished for it.

By the third inning of our first game of the season, my friend, Jay, and I each had five stolen bases. Our coach, Mark Englehart, a twenty-something who loved the game of baseball, was clearly miffed that we were taking off as soon as the pitcher was in his windup. We were not waiting for our coach's consent, a *steal signal*, a sign conveyed from the third base coach's box. We just ran. Our bodies were compelled by external forces—I ran vainly, showing off in front of Cathy; Jay ran enviously, trying to keep up with me. These were our sins. And I paid for it (as for Jay, a nonbeliever, I naturally assumed he was damned to hell for an eternity no matter what he did during the baseball game).

We were only up by one run late in the game when I strolled up to bat against the best pitcher in town, Bill "Jonesy" Jones, who was a foot taller than me, left-handed, and inserted in the game to shut us down. Jonesy had just hit a three-run homer off me in the previous inning, closing the gap to one run. Surprisingly, I was filled with anger when I stepped into the batter's box. I was overwhelmed by anger toward Jonesy for hitting the home run off me and angry at my coach for making me pitch. I had never pitched in a game before, and I had to do so in front of Cathy. I channeled my anger, determined to swing at the first pitch, even go down swinging if need be, for few had been able to get a hit off Jonesy. I had faced him many times over the years, tried every approach possible, and never once put the ball in play. He was just too damn big for his age and happened to have a father who had once played professional baseball and who enjoyed barking instructions at his son from the stands. I resolved to swing as mightily as possible and hope for the best in front of Cathy.

On the first pitch, I unleashed a mammoth swing at the baseball, which came at me with extraordinary velocity. I missed the pitch entirely; worse yet, the bat flew out of my sweaty palms and over the backstop, landing at Cathy's sandleless feet. She energetically picked up my bat and delivered it to me as I stood near the batter's box bedazzled by her beauty.

"I think you need this," she said sweetly. Her smile calmed the beast swelling within me.

Before the second pitch, I grabbed a little dirt to mix with the sweat coating my hands. Then I dug my feet into the batter's box. As Jonesy went into his windup and released the ball, I had a split second to react—a fastball was screaming toward my head. I arched my back as if I were dancing the limbo. The baseball missed my head but struck my hand, my right thumb to be exact. I fell to the ground, my body compacted, hugging my limp hand.

"Are you okay? I am sorry. I am sorry..." Jonesy kept repeating, hovering over my body.

My mother was not in the stands, yet I heard her voice: *It may hurt now, but the pain will go away. It lasts as long as or as little as you want it to.* Then I heard my ghostly father say, *Suck it up.* As I was curled on the ground, surrounded by teammates while Coach Englehart assessed the damage,

I clenched my jaw and mumbled curses at nothing and no one in particular. I would confess this sin later but not the one pertaining to my pride, which would have meant telling Father Rogers about my desire to embrace and kiss Cathy's immaculate body. When I gathered my wits and rose from the ground, my entire right arm throbbed. I peered through the crowd around me and saw Cathy. She held her hands to her nose and mouth. She was crying. But I was not. My pride fully enveloped my broken body.

After the game, Coach Englehart packed my bike into his station wagon. I did not cry from the pain until after we dropped Cathy off at her house. During the ride home, she kept looking at the bag of ice on my hand, smiling and resting her hand on my knee, which sent shockwaves through my nervous system. The physical pain mixed with pleasure turned my body rigid. I was ashamed of the baseball bat flying from my hands and of the injury, a swollen and stinging purplish-red hand like my bike, like my uniform. I was ashamed of how a damaged body made me feel so vulnerable.

Cathy was the first to sign my cast on the bus the next morning. A heavy amount of plaster crawled up my forearm to my elbow and kept my broken thumb immobile. A sling bore the weight of the cast and my humiliation, the type of embarrassment that made my speech soft and flushed my face.

"I can't believe I saw this happen to you. I thought Jonesy killed you."

"I, uh...am glad, uh...he didn't," I stuttered as she wrote the sweetest of notes on my cast: *Please don't do this again. Love, Cathy.*

It would happen again...and again...and again... I broke many bones as a teenager—my body, a reckless display of pride on various fields of play—and with each snap, chip, tear of the bone, my sister drove me to the emergency room, not my mother, whose body slowly deteriorated on the inside—the cancer gorging on her bone marrow. The chemotherapy was not healing Mom's body. She was running out of options, so she called a family meeting. It was our last.

~

It was the night before the start of my sophomore year at Corning Painted-Post West High School, which meant three things: my summer vacation had ended two weeks early because of football workouts, what we called two-a-days—excruciating practices meant to weed out the weak; I was about to start seeing the same psychologist during school weekly once again, hoping to share as little as possible but not intending to curse him; and my drinking would most likely persist—binge-worthy affairs that did not happen often, but when they did, I woke in my own piss full of shame.

"We need to have a family meeting after dinner, before school starts tomorrow." Aside from gaining a few pounds, my mother was in satisfactory spirits, spending the summer months making macrame decor with friends or reading and quoting from books by Erma Bombeck. She did not work or study at the college or sell Avon or Tupperware. Mom's body needed a respite, a rejuvenation after so much chemotherapy. Everybody understood. Mrs. Russo had drawers full of makeup, and friends had cabinets filled with Tupperware. They made no demands on my mother's remaining time on this planet.

"Oh, come on," my sister said. "What is it this time?" She was a hotshot high school senior now, captain of the girl's tennis team, undefeated on the court, and studious in the classroom, which made it difficult for me to slack off—*Christine would never act like this*, teachers quipped.

"Help me with the dishes, then we will talk." My mother

rose from the kitchen table, and the three of us followed her with our plates. I had adopted my father's habit of vigorously scraping the remains from dinner into the garbage can, cleaning the few scraps, the tiny morsels, the diminutive excess of our meal. Then I went into the family room and turned on MTV. My brother joined me. The spectacles on TV were a slow drip of Novocain before the pain of a family meeting.

"I have to get a bone marrow transplant." My mother began.

"What's that?" I snapped. The Novocain wore off quickly when I heard the word *transplant*, which made my stomach churn and ache horribly.

"It's when they take out some of my good blood and freeze it. Then the doctors give me doses of radiation that kill the bad blood. And after, the doctors put the good blood back into my body, so I won't get sick again." My mother was monotone, barely glancing at us. There was a sullenness in the way she looked at her hands as if she were reading her own palm, unsure where the lines lead.

"Take out your blood?" I was incredulous and unable to fathom such witchcraft, bloodletting, voodoo.

"Mom, when—" Chris, much like me, was stunned.

"Sometime after Christmas."

"Does Dad know?" Chris asked.

"No. You three are the first to know."

"How long—" Chris muttered.

"It's a long procedure. I'll be in the hospital a month or more. But I need to do one last chemo treatment before the bone marrow transplant."

"Who will be with us?" Chris asked.

"I plan to ask Grammy Rand."

Dusk had disappeared, replaced by a blackness painted on our sliding glass door leading from the family room to our small backyard. I sat still in a rocking chair, staring over my mother's shoulder; the blackness was beyond, surrounding our gray house. The four of us sat quietly as night settled upon us. At one end of the couch, Mom examined the future in her hands. At the other end of the couch, Chris rested her head on the palm of her left hand. In the recliner, Kev's hands were fastened to the chair as his eyes blinked rapidly. We were in the same room, the same house, same town, country, planet, but we existed in the blackness enveloping us. If the sun were to magically appear, we most certainly would have shooed it away.

I did not pray. I could not pray. I began to think four years of the same prayers going unanswered meant that God considered me unworthy, or *He* was too busy with bigger issues, such as war and famine, or *He* simply did not care. At fifteen years of age, the first seemed most plausible.

The silence in our family room was broken by our mother, who began to weep. We huddled around her and held her as she slowly poured burden after burden into her palms. She was releasing all the weight in her body—the toxic medicines and conversations, the doubts about the past and the present and the future, the certainty of waking in the morning uncertain she might not wake the next, the trust and distrust of faith and science. My mother wailed vociferously. Her agony poured from her.

The blackness overwhelming our home silenced my prayers. I had little, if any, words for God anymore as well as for my friends. I wanted to refrain from speaking unless spoken to, no longer volunteer to read in class, or raise my hand to answer questions or ask questions. My twoness started to form into a silent oneness made of bone, flesh, and blood. These were my concerns, which needed no written words or speech. If it did not have to do with the body, then I planned to discard it. I resolved to stop doing homework, talking to girls on the phone, and believing in miracles. Of course, all of this involved a degree of self-pity and naiveté, but I was young. And angry.

~

While Coach Condon was addressing the whole football team during practice one day, Brian Naida turned to me and said, "I asked Harvey Cohen, 'Did Jew get in yet?'" I smacked Brian hard in his chest protector, producing an audible *thwack!*

"Who was that?" Coach Condon boomed, perking up with pissy eyes and a frown. "Was that you, Naida?"

"No sir." Brian harnessed his laughter and elbowed me in the ribs.

"Was that you, Rand?" Coach snapped.

I lifted my head quickly, acknowledging Coach Condon's assertion.

"Rand, you have been nothing but a cancer to this team this year!"

I squinted and searched my teammates' faces, wondering if they heard the same word as I did. *Cancer.* The word drummed in my head. My body was overcome by shock and horror. It shook with incredulity, and my eyes began to well. I turned and started walking off the field of play.

"Are you quitting, Rand?" Coach Condon shouted. "That's what you are, a quitter, huh?"

Dion and Jay, Brian and John ran after me, grabbed me, and started to pull my body back onto the field. But I shook free and bolted to the locker room, where I bawled so intensely, I was on the verge of vomiting. I was a *cancer.* And unworthy of God's good graces, for my prayers went unanswered. My father was three thousand miles away, raising a young, adopted daughter, and my mother was at home, confronting her own mortality. God may have been residing somewhere in-between those two bodies, but I could not ascertain the workings of an omnipotent and omniscient being; therefore, I quit trying to make sense of divine powers. Indubitably, Coach Condon was correct. I was a quitter. Not of football. But of faith.

I was so distraught, I changed into my sneakers, threw my school clothes, cleats, and helmet into my bag, and started walking home, about a five-mile trek.

"Why are you home so early? And why are you still wearing your practice uniform, your shoulder pads?" my mother asked as soon as I walked through the front door of our gray house. "There is no bus at this time. What did you do? Did you walk home?"

I looked at my mother and started to bawl again. I tried to talk, but my mouth was full of saliva and mucus and metal braces, and my diaphragm contracted and heaved like an accordion. I was a floundering mess of a boy, a perfectly healthy body excommunicated from the field of play.

My mother grabbed me and pulled me close to her bosom. She kissed my forehead and held on to me tightly until I began to breathe regularly. She took my hand and guided me to a decrepit wicker chair in our living room.

"What happened? Start from the beginning." Mom folded her hands between her thighs and smiled.

"Coach—" I did not know what to say. I did not want to use the word Coach Condon used. I did not want to hurt my mother.

"Go ahead, Steve, tell me what is bothering you."

"Coach said," I stammered. "Coach caught me goofing off during practice." I wiped my sweaty palms on my thigh pads.

"Okay, go on, what happened next?"

"Nothing, really. He got upset."

"Well, something happened. You walked all the way home in the middle of practice."

My breathing became heavy, and I wiped the sweat from

my hands on my thigh pads again. My mother looked at me with uncertainty.

"He called me a name. Coach called me something bad. He's a jerk."

"Steve, how many times do I have to tell you, you don't call people names. You show your coaches respect." My mother shifted in her seat, crossed her legs. She wore green polyester pants and a black blouse with tan and pink flower patterns. "What name did your coach call you?"

"He said," I stammered. "He said I was *a cancer* to the team." I began to sob.

"I see," Mom replied. She stood and approached me, kissing me on the forehead, wiping tears from my face, and said, "Go get out of your practice clothes and take a shower. You'll feel better."

My mother was right. I did feel better after washing the sweat and dirt from my body. But there was a great hollowness inside me when the realization of not being able to play football for the rest of the season lodged in my mind and belly. We were only three games into the season with eight more to go, and now, because of a slap on a chest and a caustic response, I became an empty-eyed spectator who loathed the idea of watching his friends on the field of play without him.

When I walked downstairs to apologize for my behavior during practice, to tell my mother I was only trying to defend Harvey when I'd smacked Brian and it would not happen again, that I'd accept whatever punishment she deemed just, but I was really bummed I couldn't play football anymore 'cause the coach hated me, thinking I was something awful, as awful as a deadly disease, and I was sorry he called me that name, that word, called me a...

"I just got off the phone with Coach Condon. I am going to walk you over to his house. You are going to apologize to him for your behavior, and he will let you back on the team."

I stopped abruptly at the threshold to the kitchen and stood as still as the floorboards under my feet.

"What?" I asked. My shoulders were slouched like a weathered tackling dummy.

"Steve, you are going to go to Coach Condon's house with me and apologize. I am not raising a quitter. You are no quitter."

But I was.

"No, no," I pleaded. "Coach needs to apologize to me. He's the one that called me a name, called me *a cancer* to the team."

"You need to forget about what he said. He didn't mean it. He doesn't know. He could've called you many worse things."

"You mean, you think it is okay to call me *a cancer* to the team?"

"You're not *a cancer* to the team unless you choose to goof around instead of listening to your coach."

"What? I was just defending Harvey. Brian called him *a Jew.*"

"Well, tell the coach that. You should have told your coach as soon as Brian said what he said instead of causing such a ruckus."

"What? I am not telling the coach that. Brian deserved to get smacked."

"Steve, you can't go around smacking everything and everyone you don't agree with."

"I am not going with you. You can go talk to Coach Condon yourself. I am never talking to him again. He's a jerk."

"Yes, you are coming with me, young man," my mother said sternly, waving her index finger in my face. "You will apologize. And you will not quit."

She grabbed her purse and her bug-eyed sunglasses, then my hand, and we scurried out of our gray house with our hands knotted together like one of my mother's creations from macrame.

When we arrived at Coach Condon's house, my mother rang

the doorbell. He answered quickly, holding the storm door open. My mother and I stood on the top step of a short, cement staircase with black metal railings while Coach Condon stood in the middle of his doorway. He did not invite us in. We stared into each other's eyes. He may have been seething with hatred for me, but I was unequivocally filled with hatred for him.

"Thank you for making time to meet with Steve. He has something he wants to say to you." My mother was her gracious self. Then she turned to me and nodded.

"I apologize." I looked away from Coach Condon and toward my Converse high-top sneakers. "I am sorry I was goofing around. It won't happen again."

"That's good to hear. You might have to work your way back to being a starter. But if you work hard, you can do it. See you at practice tomorrow." The door swung shut, and Coach Condon disappeared.

"See that was easy now, wasn't it?" My mother slid her fingers into my hand, and we walked leisurely back to our gray house. Along the way, she stopped to greet Mrs. Huff, my friend Timmy's mother; then Mrs. Blackstone, the wife of my Scout Master; and Mrs. Gouveia, our next-door neighbor and mother of John, one of my friends who had tried to stop me from leaving the field of play only a few hours earlier.

~

FOR SEVERAL WEEKS, Coach Condon rode me hard during games and practices. I played offense and defense, kick-off and kick-return, punt-coverage and punt-return, and I held the ball for our placekicker, Chris Hogue, who was tremendously accurate, taking great pride in making field goals and not missing extra points. I never caught a break except during halftime. Luckily, Dion's mom took us out to eat after home games. I replenished myself with foot-long chili-cheese dogs and chocolate malt milkshakes.

Practices were more brutal because I did not know from one day to the next where Coach Condon was going to play me. He made me take reps with first and second teams, trying me out at a variety of positions, running our plays, running the other team's plays, or just plain running in circles on the track. It was as if Coach Condon did not know what to do with me, like I was some kind of experiment without a hypothesis.

Halfway through the season, I was asked to play running back during practice one day. My number kept getting called. I ran up the middle, off tackle, option left, option right. I was not sure where I was supposed to run specifically, so I just tried to dodge and dance around people, hoping for the best.

"Rand, stop dancing and run over somebody," Coach Condon bellowed.

Fair enough, I thought to myself. I got into the huddle. Mark "Spern Dog" Spernyak was our quarterback. He called for a quick pitch toss left. We hustled up to the line of scrimmage. The ball was snapped. Spern Dog made a perfect toss to me from five yards away as I was running toward the sideline, hoping to turn the corner and run as far and as fast up the field as my body propelled me. But Fred Hemly, who was unblocked, charged at me. He was one of the best tacklers on our defense, weighed at least fifty pounds more than me, and had a great angle to stop me. Typically, I liked to spin around guys bigger than me in a one-on-one situation. Sometimes it worked. Sometimes it did not. At least, if I spun quickly, a relatively harmless arm tackle might bring my body to the ground instead of the full force from a more hulking body than mine. But coach's suggestion to *run over somebody* was rattling in my head, and, unfortunately, the whole team had heard Coach Condon say this; subsequently, Fred came at me low, below the waist, below the knees, so low the crown of his helmet hit me directly on my right ankle. The impact forced a ligament to tear free from a bone in my body, tearing part of my ankle bone free from my leg bone. A devastating injury. Deservedly so since I was *a cancer* to the team.

When my sister pulled the brown battleship into our school's parking lot to pick me up, I hopped to the car on one leg with ice tightly wrapped against my ankle by an ace bandage. Chris climbed out of the car.

"What did you do?" she hollered immediately.

I just kept hopping toward her. When I arrived at the car, I opened the passenger door and sat down.

"Let me take a look." My sister knelt on one knee, carefully holding the calf of my injured leg while unwrapping the ace bandage. I sat sideways in the passenger seat, wincing, dangling one leg above the asphalt while my sister took great care with the other leg. Her candy-striping experience was a great relief for my brother and me.

"Geez, Steve, how did this happen?"

I looked down. My right ankle, if you want to call it that, looked more like a decayed log, thick and black with hints of green hues. My sister examined the damage to my body.

"Geez, we have to get you to the emergency room. Mom's gonna be upset when she hears about this. Let's wait a few days before we tell her, okay?"

I nodded.

"Who did this to you?"

"I was trying to run over Fred Hemly."

"Geez, Steve, he's twice your size. What were you thinking?"

I shrugged.

~

I was on crutches for two months. During this time, my sister reminded me daily that she was not going to take care of me while Mom was in the hospital and that Gram was not going to take care of me either. But my mother thought otherwise when we talked by phone: *Your sister will help you out, just tell her what you need.* My mother heaped this burden of two reckless brothers on my sister's conscience once again, a weighty, unfair expectation, forcing my sister to be chauffeur, head chef, nurse, student, tennis captain, taskmaster, and, when time permitted, a friend to many. My sister leaned heavily on her girlfriends, choosing to confide in them, unburdening herself, opening up to them instead of Father Rogers. She embraced the healing power of sisterhood instead of confessing her pain and suffering to a priest in a confessional. Frankly, Father Rogers could not offer the countenance my sister desperately needed. As a singularly minded man of the cloth, he was ill-equipped to comprehend the intricacies of sisterhood and how such bonds were born from tribulations of unreasonable expectations thrust upon women for millennia.

Normally, I walked a half mile to the bus stop with my friends. Since I had to hobble about to-and-fro on crutches, my sister, under the direct orders of my mother, dutifully drove me to school. She was slightly resentful, mostly protective, not wanting me to harm my body anymore, wishing I were *The Boy in The Plastic Bubble*, relegated to a plexiglass room for a lifetime, or wishing I were in a sealed box marked *fragile* and placed on a dusty shelf. With these thoughts in mind, my sister often advised me to stop being a *klutz*, which I considered a term of endearment.

Chris had to cart me around in the brown battleship because I was required to attend football practices, along with games, where I cheered on my teammates, perfunctorily showing signs of interest in a sport I had once loved before I was labeled a *cancer* by Coach Condon. Most of my time on crutches was spent searching for the cheerleading squad, hoping to catch glimpses of the senior girls, my sister's friends, doing routines during practices or games. These were innocent crushes I was hoping to turn into dalliances, fantasies of a hobbled fifteen-year-old boy with broken bones.

Eventually, I had to set aside the fantasy of dating a senior cheerleader so I could focus on two things: sobriety and a raunchy smell emitting from my cast. After only a few weeks of wearing three pounds of plaster, my leg and foot became itchy and downright foul. A rash had formed, so I carried a wooden ruler in my backpack, using it to scratch my skin wrapped in plaster. It was like mashing potatoes. My arm became a jackhammer hitting the skin between my toes, under my foot, my shin, and the back of my calf all at once. Then I would pour Johnson & Johnson baby powder down my leg and ankle to mask the stench, powdering my foot as well as my toes. I scratched and scratched during Algebra, during lunch, during study hall and World History. I was a hot mess of a body without control. The most painful aspect of a rotting log of a leg was that I had to sacrifice two new pairs of Wrangler pants, cutting one pant leg off each so I could slide the thick cast through a short-like fashion above my knees. Since I only owned three pairs of pants, I was down to one pair for the remainder of the school year. Luckily, my Aunt Pat sent large boxes of hand-me-downs; her three sons and daughter provided us with plenty of clothes to grow into. I rummaged through those boxes in our cellar and found corduroy pants that were roomy but functional as the days got colder. I had to cinch a gray macrame belt my mother had made like a tourniquet to keep these pants from falling. I felt far less guilty cutting one leg off these pants.

Although the cast was cumbersome and smelly, I did my best to bounce around like a hip-hop-dancing novice, a sign of the times. My body slid into desks, cars, church pews easily, bounded down and launched upstairs energetically, avoided collisions in the school's hallways, and avoided the confessional while my mother remained in the hospital, receiving the last of her chemotherapy regimen before the bone marrow transplant. When she called and asked, *How is the ankle?*—I wished to say, *My punishment was not as severe as yours.* Instead, I mumbled vague words that I barely heard.

I did not call my father after the injury. I figured if he wanted to know how I was doing, he would make the effort, which was a rarity that summer, that fall, that winter. Then he showed up in the spring, silent and injured like me.

~

ONE DAY WE DID NOT HAVE FOOTBALL PRACTICE after school, so Jerry Stilwell invited the team and the cheerleading squad, among others, over to his house. I had told my sister and Gram I was going to catch a ride home with friends. We all rode the school bus to Jerry's place. His parents were still at work. Before long, the liquor cabinet was raided, and bottles were being passed around. Just about everyone drank.

The following day, Coach Condon asked the team to not bother dressing for practice and to meet with the other coaches and him in the gym.

"It has come to my attention that there was a party after school yesterday and that people were drinking alcohol," Coach Condon began, to our astonishment. "Consuming alcohol is against school policy and grounds for immediate dismissal from a sports team. We are going to meet with every player individually, and I want to know where the alcohol came from and who was drinking it."

As we waited to be interrogated, my teammates, my friends,

argued vehemently with each other about whether to tell the truth—we all were drinking—or not.

It was an easy decision for me. My season was over. But I had decided on telling one harmless lie before I entered the interrogation room.

"So, Rand, were you drinking?" Coach Condon asked. Other coaches were in the room as well. It was dark, only a few chairs and a table.

"Yes."

"Thought so. Who else was drinking?"

"Just me."

"Naida said he was drinking. Are you saying he was not?"

"If he said he was, then he was."

"Who else was drinking?"

"Just Naida and me."

"No one else?"

"Nope."

"You sure? We know others were drinking."

I nodded but remained silent.

"Okay, have it your way." Coach Condon wore frustration on his face. "You are no longer allowed to participate in our football program. You need to turn in your gear and uniform. You're off the team."

Brian and I turned our gear and uniforms in together. I dragged mine in a large mesh bag behind me, holding onto the bag's long drawstring as I moved with my crutches. We did not talk as the team manager checked off all the gear. We were in a narrow corridor. Brian leaned against a wall and began shaking his head. His eyes welled with tears as he fought against his heartbreak.

"Fucking assholes. None of them have the balls to admit they drank."

I leaned on my crutches, looking at Brian. He was in a painful place. I, on the other hand, felt a sense of relief. I no longer felt like *a cancer* to the team. I was excised like a malignant tumor.

~

Charles Morrell, my grandfather, finished off the last of his paperwork then scooped up his fourteen-year-old daughter, Dorothy, and her crutches. The metal brace on one leg clanged as he carried her back out into the wintry afternoon of December 18, 1944. Once again, he patiently and gently slid Dorothy and her crutches into the Nash 600. The snowfall had subsided—a few flurries flung into Dorothy's view out of the car window—while the car crept up the hill to Heaton Hospital, a slow and slushy drive along the streets of Montpelier, Vermont.

At approximately 4:00 p.m., Charles and Dorothy heard the cry of a newborn from Florence's hospital room. They were waiting excitedly near the door. Charles held his fedora with both hands while Dorothy held a rosary tightly to her chest with both of her hands. She had prayed for a baby sister. Her prayers were heard.

"I want you to meet your baby sister, Anne," Florence said to Dorothy, who had to enter the room slowly or the wooden crutches smacked against the black boots and metal leg brace. Dorothy was awestruck by the size of Anne, the tininess of her hands, the two paper cuts for eyes, the two slivers for dimples. She did not remember when her younger brother was born, but she remembered Anne's birth for a lifetime. She held Anne's diminutive body for hours while Florence rested and prayed. Charles gently kissed Anne's forehead while Dorothy cradled the baby in her lap. Then he returned to work.

Florence chose the baby's name because of her fondness for a shrine on Isle La Motte in Northern Vermont. Saint Anne's

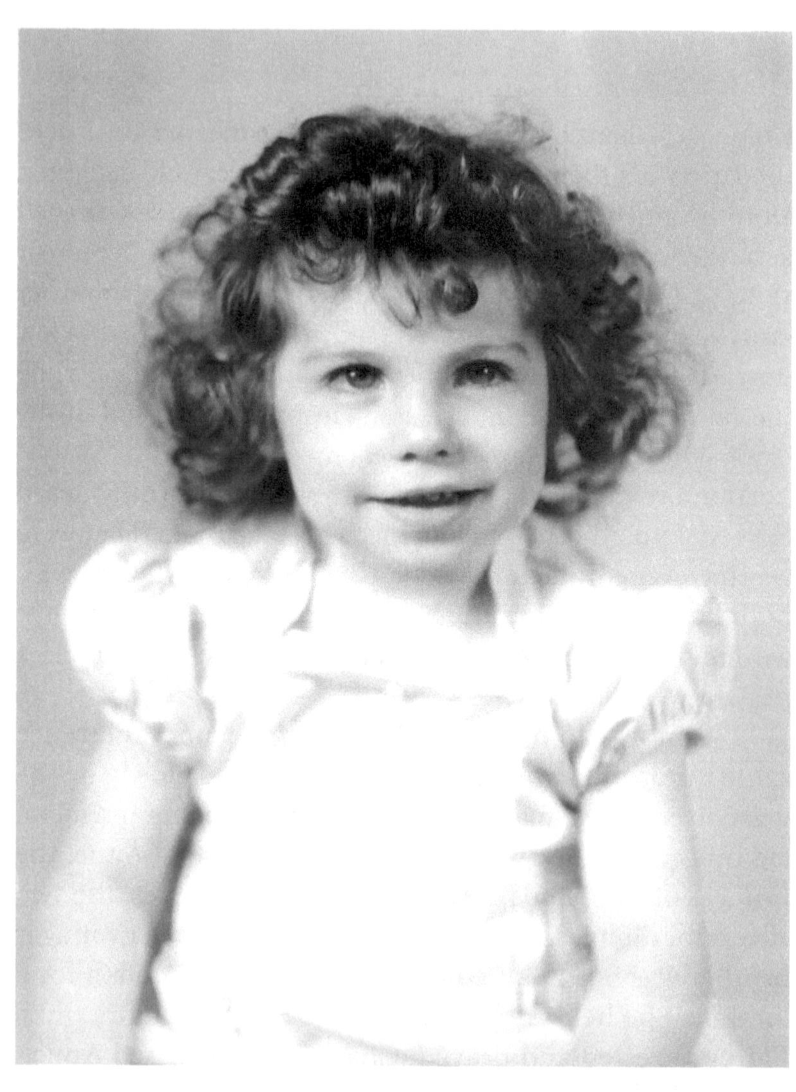

Shrine was constructed in 1666 as a fort and chapel, established for the purpose of trade and the conversion of native people. By the time Florence started visiting the shrine as a child, it had been transformed into a place for Catholic pilgrims who sought solace and a spiritual awakening on a bucolic island, which rested near the border of Vermont and New York along the pristine shores of Lake Champlain.

~

At the shrine on Isle La Motte there is a statue of Saint Anne, the mother of Mary, with the inscription: *Remember Dismas the good thief of calvary*. According to the Bible, Dismas was one of two thieves hanging on a cross next to Jesus. He asked if he could join Jesus in Heaven. According to the Gospels, Jesus quickly responded, *You will join me in paradise.*

Whether my mother forgave my father before she died will never be known. Whether she reconciled the fact that she would not live long enough to be a grandmother, like Saint Anne, will never be known. Whether she entered the paradise she longed for will never be known. What is known is that she died alone at Roswell Park Comprehensive Cancer Center in Buffalo, New York, on March 9, 1984.

~

I was upstairs in my room, reading *Pet Sematary* by Stephen King. Baseball tryouts had just started, and Lou Condon happened to be the baseball coach, too. I was still bitter about his careless language and general rudeness, but I loved baseball so much I worked up the courage to approach Coach Condon in the gym one afternoon. "Coach, should I try out for baseball?"

Admittedly, I thought enough time had lapsed since I had

been kicked off the football team for drinking alcohol, but I was unsure if Coach Condon felt the same or if he held any resentment. I was so nervous I had to wipe my sweaty palms vigorously on my pant legs, and I was immensely surprised when he said, "Sure. That's a good idea." I nodded and walked away, grinning and giddy like the day I showed my Little League coach the first baseman's mitt sent from California. There was a soft rap on the open door. Dusk was peeking through the window, winking shadows, quieting the last days of winter. I craned my neck. Gram entered my bedroom. She was wearing an apron. Unlike my mother, Gram had no qualms about my taste in books. If she knew of their contents, she may have protested, like my mother, who was opposed to the fearful and violent scenes: people losing limbs, people dying horrible deaths, people possibly losing their once unshakable faith. But I doubt Gram had any interest in a book titled *Pet Sematary*, an unromantic title, not *Harlequin* enough. Conversely, my heart raced while turning the pages of Stephen King's books, imagining, desperately hoping, his heroes survive and overcome their worst fears. I never recalled a moment when Gram expressed fear during the years she watched over us. Her gate was slow, and her tone was soft as she approached me. "Stevie, I need you to go downstairs. Your mom's friends are here." Gram's eyes were bloodshot and watery.

Kev and Chris were sitting on the rickety wicker furniture with Joyce Hollenbeck, a stout woman younger than my mother, and Pat Landsdowne, a willowy woman of similar age as my mother, in our living room. They were waiting quietly for Gram and me.

"Your mother has taken a turn for the worse. We are going to go see her, and we thought Chris should go to the hospital with us," Joyce said. Pat sat next to her, weeping and wiping her nose with a balled-up tissue.

"I think Steve should go, too," my sister said before I was able to make the request.

"I wanna go," Kev said.

"No, dearie, I need you here with me," Gram said while standing next to Kev, patting him on his head. Kev, at this juncture of his life, only obeyed three people on the planet—Bump, Nanny, and Gram—thankfully.

"Okay, Steve, Chris, go get your stuff, and we'll get going. It is going to be a long drive," Joyce said while Pat wiped tears from her eyes.

I was not sure what to pack, so I threw a Rubik's Cube, the novel I was reading, a Walkman, a couple of Styx cassettes, and a jacket into my backpack.

"Steve, you mind giving this to Mom?"

I turned around. My brother stood before me with an outstretched hand holding onto a green envelope. I took it from his hand.

"Sure." I put the envelope into my backpack.

Joyce and Pat were waiting at the front door for Chris and me. Joyce was smiling and Pat was composed when we came down the stairs. We shuffled out of the gray house and into a dark night without clouds. Joyce drove a large, cream-colored Chrysler, which handled much like our brown battleship. It drifted onto the highway and into the darkness methodically. Few cars were heading west.

I turned on my Walkman, keeping my eyes on the sky, imagining another world beyond the stars, wishing my brother was with me, wishing I did not have to deliver his envelope. I wondered why Joyce and Pat wanted only Chris to go, and why Gram wanted Kev to stay with her. The car hummed along the highway calmly. No one talked. I was numb, and the world was too dark to read.

When we arrived at the hospital there were many lights

illuminating the parking lot. Roswell Park Comprehensive Cancer Center was a large facility, so it took us a while to find Mom's room. She was in the intensive care unit.

The only other time I had seen my mother in a hospital was when my father brought the three of us to visit her after a surgery to remove tumors. The three of us had been in elementary school at the time. We had sat in four-legged chairs, our feet dangling like ornaments on a tree, watching our mother resting while our father had sat, looking at his hands. He had been quiet. Then he had softly said, "Your mother is sick." And that was all he had said. He had returned to studying his meshed fingers and open palms as if he had been reading the story of his life in each wrinkle. His teeth were disappearing at the time, and so was his ability to care for anyone other than himself, an erosion of faith and loyalty. Selfishness and fear had seemed to be infecting his heart. What else would a scared young boy believe while staring at his pigeon-toed feet in a hospital room while his father refused to offer a single word of comfort to his children or his wife?

~

"Chris, maybe Steve and you should go in the room alone. Pat and I will wait for you out here," Joyce said, and Pat nodded in agreement, her eyes swelled with tears.

We did as they asked. The first thing that captured my attention as I approached my mother's body was the framed "Footprints in the Sand" poem on an end table next to her bed. She brought this poem, housed in a wooden frame, to the hospital every time she had a surgery or chemotherapy regimen and for the bone marrow transplant. When she was not in the hospital, the framed poem hung on our kitchen wall in our gray house.

Before she left to go to the hospital one last time, my mother explained to me what the "Footprints in the Sand" poem meant to her: "I love this poem because it gives me strength and peace to know God is nearby, and I do believe God has picked me up and carried me or else I would not have made it this far. I would not have lived this long. I would not have endured this disease for as long as I have. I would not have been able to see you grow into a man, if not for the grace of God."

~

TECHNICALLY, MY MOTHER'S DEATH WAS AN ACCIDENT. She slipped and fell near the doorway of her room, slamming her head so hard against the floor she suffered a traumatic brain injury. She immediately fell into a coma and was placed on life support.

Before she fell, her body had been weakened and bruised and swollen from high doses of radiation. It never had the chance to accept or reject a transplant of her own healthy marrow that was stored in a freezer, waiting to replenish a fatigued body.

Mysteriously, Mom had risen from her bed and walked unassisted before the fall. Maybe she had risen from her bed because of a parched throat yearning for a glass of water... Maybe she had risen because of a full bladder yearning for relief... Maybe she had risen because of an empty stomach yearning for nourishment... Maybe she had risen out of habit because her thirteen-year crusade against cancer had compelled her to walk alone in a room with only a prayer in a frame nearby... Maybe she had risen because she had wanted to pray in the hospital's chapel instead of her bed... Maybe she had risen, believing God planned to carry her beleaguered body to the sea... Maybe she had risen, dreaming of a heavenly paradise outside her door... Maybe she had risen and felt faint after a few steps... Maybe she had risen and her knees buckled under her weight... Yet she had risen. Alone.

There must have been confusion and shock when the nurse or doctor had found her on the floor. They must have questioned the motive: Why rise and walk alone after so much radiation was pumped into the body, after so much marrow was extracted from the body?

No one had told my sister or me about the fall, the brain injury or coma, before we entered our mother's room.

~

THE SECOND THING I NOTICED was the corrugated tube down my mother's throat and the dried blood at the corners of her lips. Her chest rose and fell rhythmically, normally. I was not attuned to the machinery generating her breath.

"Mom, Mom." I held her hand. It was warm and bruised; deep green and purple marks dotted her arms. "Mom, Mom."

The room was large and extremely bright. I saw everything: the freckles on her neck, strings of gray atop her head, reddish blotches on her temples, a white sheet and light blue blanket pulled tight to her chest, which surged and collapsed much like my body. But she could not hear me, so I ran to the other side of her bed and held her other hand, also riddled with green-blue spots.

"Mom! Mom!" Maybe I was too quiet, so I raised my voice. I grabbed her shoulder and tried to shake her awake.

"Mom! Mom!" I yelled. "Wake up!"

I didn't know how to wake her. I looked at my sister. She stood at the end of the bed. Her hands rested on one of Mom's legs, and her face was crimson and confused.

"Chris, why won't she wake up? What is going on? Why doesn't she hear me?"

My sister wasn't answering me. I began to pace back and forth. Then I decided to place my mouth close to my mother's cheek. I held her hand once again.

"Mom, Mom, please wake up. Please, please wake up."

Then I felt hands on my shoulders pulling me away from my mother. I turned and saw that it was a strange woman in blue scrubs, a nurse.

"She can't hear you," she said.

"What? What do you mean?" I shook free from her grasp and returned to my mother's side.

"Mom! Mom! Can you hear me? Can you hear me? It's Steve, your son! Mom! Mom!"

Many hands suddenly grabbed me, and the room began feeling too small, too bright, too painful. I began to swing my elbows and fists and kick and claw.

"Leave him alone!" my sister screamed. "He doesn't know what is going on!" She started to push the nurses and orderlies.

There were four people trying to corral my wild body as I continued punching and twisting and kicking.

"Please! Please! Let go of him! He doesn't know! He doesn't know!"

My sister pulled me away and wrapped her arms around me. She was bawling and hugging me tightly, preventing my arms and legs from moving, refusing to release me. The bright lights were hurting my eyes. Like a brilliant sun, the lights bore into me, making my whole body tremble and sting.

"Let's go to the chapel, Steve." Chris released me, grabbed my hand and led us both away from the disturbing light and our mother's lifeless body. "It will make us feel better."

~

THE HOSPITAL CHAPEL WAS NOT FAR from the intensive care unit. When Chris pulled the glass door open and we entered, I immediately noticed the rear wall behind the tabernacle was freshly painted and the smell of frankincense and myrrh was absent. There was a large, gilded statue of Christ surrounded by vases of various colored faux flowers in front of the altar. Palm tree leaves were spread like fans behind the faux flowers. It was the smallest chapel I had ever been in, only a few rows of empty pews. There were glass walls on three sides, so praying was not a private matter.

We knelt in the first pew. I folded my hands together, but words, let alone sentences, were not forming in my mind. I could not recall Our Lord's Prayer, an incantation that had suddenly vanished from memory. My palms were sweaty. I could only conjure streaks of bright white light.

The chapel began to feel small, constricting. I focused on the gilded Christ who wore a solemn expression; his hands were outstretched with his palms up. I felt it was insincere and lacking compassion, an apathetic look of someone without wisdom, without moxie. For years I gazed upon renderings of Christ strewn about the churches I prayed in, always portrayed as the sorrowful one, a powerless figure who did not fight.

I stood and walked directly to the gilded statue. I looked into the eyes of Christ, pointed my index finger in its face—its sorrowful, pitiful face.

"Fuck you!" I yelled. "Fuck you!"

Chris wrapped her arms around me from behind and pressed her head into my shoulders. She had a firm grasp of my body.

"Fuck you! Fuck you!" I roared and wailed and raged at the statue.

Chris held on, hugging me tightly, locking her hands together firmly, pinning my arms, constricting my legs, grounding my body before Christ. Her tears fell on my shoulder, and she began to rock me like a child, quieting me with sob-filled shushes, *shshshshshsh...*

Footprints

The constant rhythm of the ocean
the constant rhythm of her walk
allows hearts to beat in unison
as they wash away the rooted rock

In a singular step toward divinity
a wave of unknown strength crashes
along young sand and old memories
as each deep footprint vanishes

And so she walks along the shore
remembering a time without affliction
scarred and lonely she will be no more
seeking solace to relinquish her burden

Of a youthful body sun-spoiled and poisoned
adrift across cosmic seas full of brilliant light
that strikes harmoniously
becoming a blessed prayer like song

ACKNOWLEDGMENTS

Thank you Tom Powers, Barbara Kreiger, and Gary Lenhart (posthumously) for being wonderful readers. I am indebted to my family historians: my Aunt Dot (posthumously) and Aunt Joy, along with my cousins Casey, Jane, and Patti. Much love goes to my extended family for providing history and honesty. Thank you to the team at Onion River Press: Rachel Carter, Riley Earle, and Rachel Fisher. Shout out to Chris Whalen for his practical advice, Kenny Logan for his prescient insights, Kate Haughey for her tremendous compassion, Jason Marzini for his passion and encouragement, Jamie Gage for his wit and wile, Tedin Lange for her vast and informative sticky notes throughout the manuscript, Jared and Kathy Cadwell for their tremendous kindness and enthusiasm, and Mo Shea for her cheerleading, sincerity and eternal wisdom. Shout out to my friends and colleagues who are always so brilliantly optimistic during trying times.

There have been many blessings in my life, mainly the enduring love of family. Although my wife, Wendy, enjoys a sandy beach, she is the *rock*. Our children, Gabe, Jake, Molly, and Thayer, continue to mesmerize, along with our grandchildren, Hallie, Nolan, and Taylor. A special thanks to Ben and Haley for being part of our family. Lastly, I am indebted to my siblings—thank you, along with much love for my niece, Josie, and my nephews, Eli and Matthew.

Steve Rand is an author and director for civic engagement at Norwich University. After serving in the Navy as a photographer, he studied English, history, and education at the University of Vermont, where he won a writing award, the UVM Allbee Award for Excellence in Writing. He has a Master of Arts in Liberal Studies from Dartmouth College. His focus of study was creative writing and cultural studies. He and his wife live in Vermont. They have four children and three grandchildren. Steve enjoys skiing, mountain biking, and hiking.